FORMAL SEMANTICS OF PROGRAMMING LANGUAGES

**Prentice-Hall
Series in Automatic Computation**

George Forsythe, editor

COURANT
COMPUTER SCIENCE
SYMPOSIUM 2
SEPTEMBER 14-16, 1970

FORMAL SEMANTICS OF PROGRAMMING LANGUAGES

Edited by **RANDALL RUSTIN**

Courant Institute of Mathematical Sciences
New York University

PRENTICE-HALL, INC., Englewood Cliffs, New Jersey

ISBN: 0-13-329060-3

Library of Congress Catalog Card No.: 75-39372

10 9 8 7 6 5 4 3 2 1

Printed in the United States of America

PRENTICE-HALL INTERNATIONAL, INC., London
PRENTICE-HALL OF AUSTRALIA, PTY. LTD., Sydney
PRENTICE-HALL OF CANADA, LTD., Toronto
PRENTICE-HALL OF INDIA PRIVATE LIMITED, New Delhi
PRENTICE-HALL OF JAPAN, INC., Tokyo

CONTENTS

Foreword
Introduction
Participants

Jacob T. Schwartz
*Semantic Definition Methods and the
Evolution of Programming Languages*   1

Wayne T. Wilner
*Formal Semantic Definition Using
Synthesized and Inherited Attributes*   25

Peter Lucas
*On the Semantics of Programming
Languages and Software Devices*   41

Calvin C. Elgot
Remarks on One-Argument Program Schemes   59

Dana Scott
Lattice Theory, Data Types and Semantics   65

J. H. Morris, Jr.
*A Correctness Proof Using Recursively
Defined Functions*   107

Ralph L. London
*A Correctness Proof of the Fisher-Galler
Algorithm Using Inductive Assertions*   125

John McCarthy
*Formal Semantic Definition and the
Proof of Compiler Correctness*   137

Clement L. McGowan
*An Inductive Proof Technique for
Interpreter Equivalence*   139

Peter Wegner
Programming Language Semantics   149

A. van Wijngaarden
Constructive Formalization   249

FOREWORD

The series of books of which the present volume is the second originated in a symposium series in areas of current interest in computer science which were presented by the Computer Science Department of the Courant Institute of Mathematical Sciences of New York University. Participants and speakers were drawn from the academic and industrial communities to allow the interchange of ideas between these two groups. The participants were selected for knowledge of and active involvement in the fields to be discussed.

The emphasis at the meeting was on the discussion of open problems rather than on presentation of solved problems. References for greater detail have been appended to the papers.

Written versions of the talks were not submitted prior to the meeting. Speakers had the option of editing their transcripts or providing written equivalents. It should be clear which papers are most faithful to the spoken word. The atmosphere of the meetings was intended to be informal, and discussion was encouraged by allocating time for question periods and breaks after each talk.

Support for the meetings was provided by a grant from the Mathematics Program of the Office of Naval Research. I would like to thank Dr. Leila Bram for her interest in and involvement with the symposia; and Professor Jacob T. Schwartz for the general conception of the series and the choice of specific topics.

I would also like to express my gratitude to Ms Linda Adamson, without whose typing and editing assistance this volume would not exist; and to Ms Connie Engle, without whose administrative and organizational help I fear the symposium would not have existed.

                    Randall Rustin
                    Administrator of the Symposia

INTRODUCTION

This introduction is intended to orient the reader who may be familiar with aspects of the formal semantics of programming languages, but not specifically the work of the participants in this volume.

Jacob Schwartz surveys methods of semantic specification in the first part of his talk. This material is valuable as an introduction to the subject matter of the meeting. Further on, Professor Schwartz speculates on the future direction of programming languages. He predicts greater development of what he terms "languages of mechanism," or "object-describing languages," as opposed to the more usual computational languages. The former provide the means for the declaration of objects and their combination; the latter provide for: sequenced execution, combination of functions, and assignment for preserving the results of function evaluation. For illustration, a language of mechanism is described and examples of its use are presented.

Peter Lucas traces the historical background which led to the activities of the IBM Vienna Laboratory in the formal definition of PL/I. His primary concern is the systematic design and proof of correctness of implementations based on formal language definitions. The language definition in this approach is given by the interpreter for the specified abstract machine. Study of particular features is done by study of the corresponding parts of the abstract machine. The proof of correctness of the implementation of a language feature is established by demonstrating that a specified equivalence relation holds between the defining interpreter and the implementation. A tutorial example of the "twin-machine" technique for proving correctness for a particular software device (a stack) is presented in detail.

John McCarthy's work was seminal for that of the Vienna group, as well as for that of a

considerable number of workers in the field of
formal semantics. At the meeting he presented a
tutorial and review of this work for which references are given in this volume.

Wayne Wilner's paper, which is an extension of
work by Don Knuth, has been placed early in this
volume because the approach to semantic specification presented might be more intuitively accessible
to those familiar with formal syntactic specification methods. The value of the parse tree of the
input string is built of local values, i.e., with
attributes which have been assigned to each of the
terminal and non-terminal symbols of the grammar.
This information is passed up and down the tree
by what are described in the paper as synthesized
and inherited attributes respectively. The talk
closes with a discussion of a compiler constructed
with this technique.

Jim Morris and Ralph London present solutions
to the same problem using different techniques of
proof. Each, however, considers the value computed
by the program the result of a functional transformation applied to the input values. The value
obtained on execution of the program must then be
proved correct in some specified formal sense.

Ralph London came to the meeting as a partici-
pant, not as a speaker. As a direct result of a
discussion he had with Jim Morris at the meeting he
attempted the proof which appears in this volume.
Since one of the hopes of the symposium series was
that it be something of a catalyst for further
research, it was particularly gratifying to include
Dr. London's paper in this proceedings.

Calvin Elgot presents a brief intuitive discussion of a mathematically precise description of a
limited class of program schemes. The work was
intended as an introduction to a more detailed
mathematical presentation, the reference to which
is contained in the paper.

Dana Scott outlines a general theory of

approximation. The approximation relation is chosen
to be a partial ordering in which limits exist.
With other considerations attended to, the mathematical objects realized by the limits result in complete spaces on lattices. Function spaces can be
the result of this construction and the values
obtained can be used for semantic interpretation of
programming languages.

The last paper in the volume, Peter Wegner's,
advances the operational approach to programming
language semantics, and extensively compares the
applicability of this technique with other approaches.
He presents detailed examples of the methods of proof
favored by him, and Clem McGowan who has collaborated
with Dr. Wegner in this work. The paper is the most
extensive in its historical scope and may be profitably read as a survey, with critical commentary, of
other work in the field.

Clement McGowan deals specifically with techniques which are viable for the proof of the correctness of the execution of any program in a particular
language implementation. If the semantics of the
language is defined by an abstract interpreter, then
we wish to know if a program in the implemented
language computes the same result as the abstract
interpreter applied to that program. When the actual
implementation is interpretive, then the proof of its
correctness depends on a technique for proving interpreter equivalence. McGowan presents an inductive
proof technique for establishing this equivalence.

Professor A. van Wijngaarden's talk has unfortunately not been included in this volume. Due to
technical recording problems it was lost. References to his and other work concerning ALGOL 68 are,
however, included here.

Randall Rustin

PARTICIPANTS

Allen, Frances	IBM
Amoroso, S.	Stevens Institute of Technology
Andrieu, Joyce	Allen-Babcock Computing, Inc.
Beidler, John A.	University of Scranton
Berry, Dan	Brown University
Blum, E.K.	University of Southern Calif.
Ching, S.W.	Villanova University
Christopher, T.W.	Inst. for Computer Research
de Bokker, J.W.	Mathematisch Centrum, Amsterdam
Fisher, Jr., G.A.	Illinois Inst. of Technology
Gerhart, Susan	Carnegie-Mellon University
Haggerty, J.P.	Bell Telephone Labs., Whippany
Harrison, Michael A.	University of California
Hochberg, Mark	Columbia University
Hwang, Rosa C.	University of Pennsylvania
Igarashi, Shigeru	Kyoto Univ. & Stanford Univ.
Joshi, Aravind K.	University of Pennsylvania
Kieburtz, R.B.	S.U.N.Y., Stonybrook
Levy, Leon S.	University of Delaware
Landin, Peter J.	Queen Mary College, U. of London
London, Ralph L.	University of Wisconsin
Loveman, David B.	Air Force Inst. of Technology
Mezei, Jorge	IBM
Montieri, Dr.	Carnegie-Mellon University
Morris, Jr., J.H.	University of California
Murphy, Janet E.	M.I.T.
Nummi, Veli J.	University of Toronto, Canada
Ostrinsky, R.	Brooklyn College
Ringquist, Barbara	U.S. Air Force, Oklahoma
River, Eleanor	M.I.T.
Schneider, Victor B.	Purdue University
Sethi, Ravi	IBM
Snyder, Larry	Carnegie-Mellon University
Sondak, Norman E.	Worcester Polytechnic Institute
Stark, R.H.	New Mexico State University
Tsao, John H.	IBM
Villarino, Mark B.	University of Kentucky
Walk, K.	IBM Vienna, Austria
Weyuker, Elaine J.	Richmond College, C.U.N.Y.
Zalcstein, Yechezkel	Carnegie-Mellon University

FORMAL
SEMANTICS
OF
PROGRAMMING
LANGUAGES

SEMANTIC DEFINITION METHODS AND THE EVOLUTION OF PROGRAMMING LANGUAGES

Jacob T. Schwartz
Courant Institute of Mathematical Sciences
New York University

Various principal methods used for semantic specification are briefly surveyed. To illuminate the problems to which semantic specification tools must be applied, a distinction between two types of programming languages, the computational and the object-describing, is proposed and illustrated. This leads to certain general anticipations concerning the future development of programming languages.

In the present talk, intended to be introductory, I shall dwell discursively on three points. First, I shall describe, from my own point of view, the general problem with which this seminar is concerned; then I'll make a few introductory remarks about the methods potentially available for dealing with these problems, i.e., the methods which can aid in the "semantic" definition of programming languages. Finally, I shall speculate concerning the future development of programming languages; such speculation can, if one is lucky, help to depict the substantive matter to which semantic definition — a tool — must eventually be applied.

On the first point: syntactic specification
serves to define a class of strings -- the valid programs of a particular language. Semantic specification, on the other hand, defines a *value* for each
valid program. Here the word value is used in a
very general sense; the value of a program need not
necessarily be a single number or a highly unitary
object, but may, for example, be the entire history
of the computation associated with the program --
its abstract trace, if you will. Thus, syntax is
the definition of a class of programs, semantics
the definition of a value function over this class.
The definitional problem to be faced may be very
complex, in that a programming language may incorporate a great variety of disparate features, relating it to highly varied application areas. Think,
for example, of PL/1!

The first part of the language definition
problem, syntactic definition, has by now been much
and successfully studied. We can confidently regard
syntactic analysis as a process which carries us
from an external "source string" representation of
a program to an internal representation whose details
are intended to facilitate the semantic definition
process which is to follow. We know how to summarize
the result of syntactic program analysis using a
parse tree or *syntax tree*. We know a variety of
algorithms usable in this area, and understand the
structure of these algorithms sufficiently well
to describe them by summary *metalanguages*, thereby
obtaining a decisive symbolic representation
of the syntactic definition/analysis process. We
have sufficient confidence in our understanding of
syntactic analysis to be willing to make the outcome
of syntactic analysis, namely the syntax tree representation of a program, into a standard starting
point for our thinking on program semantics. Therefore, we may take the semantic problem to be that
of associating a value, in the general sense described above, with each *abstract program*,, i.e.,
parse tree.

The step to be taken next is, however, much
less well understood. Let me attempt to summarize

the definitional methods available for treatment of the semantic problem that must be faced. I will list methods both formal and informal as long as they embody an idea worth noting.

A first method, familiar to all from experience with programming language manuals, and definitely informal, is the descriptive definition of program meaning using natural language, i.e., English. Note that in giving such definitions one might hope, by being extremely systematic, to attain rigor to the degree normal for any sort of mathematical definition. An inescapable difficulty lies, however, in the fact that programming languages with all their parts are structures considerably more complex than those studied in mathematics; the necessity of coping with all this complexity casts doubt over the definitional adequacy for this purpose of natural language. Note also that what one finds in a pro-gramming language manual is almost never a systematic formal definition of the meaning of programs. Instead, one finds a definition having a strongly expository flavor, in which certain salient features may be set forth with relative care, but in which much is suggested rather than stated and left for the reader, guided by certain principles of natural-ness and minimum surprise, to supply by deduction. Various obvious objections to such a definitional method arise; and the strongest of these objections applies even to hypothetical attempts to use natural language in a rigorous, completely systematic way. This objection is as follows: natural language itself incorporates a huge and unanalyzed body of tools, and we are still so far from being able to treat natural language mechanically, especially in regard to its own semantic properties, that we have no mechanical way of processing natural language definitions. That is, even if given what purports to be a complete natural language definition D of a programming language L, we have no programmable way either of verifying the completeness of D, or of mechanically transforming D into a compiler or an interpreter for L, or of mechanically determining whether any given compiler for L does realize the object defined by D. A definitional scheme ideally should aid us to rise from simplicity to complexity, and therefore a metalanguage should be simpler than the language which it is used to define; in this lies an inescapable objection to the use of natural language as a semantic specification tool.

The second semantic definition method commonly encountered, and one suitable for either informal or for formal use, is that which may be called the method of *devolution*. This is a method which has been used formally and systematically in ALGOL 68, but which as an informal method is much older. The method is as follows: within a language L to be defined semantically, we specify a sublanguage λ, as restricted as possible; then we treat the full language L as an extension of λ. That is, specifying some formal mechanism by which programs written in L can be replaced by programs written in the more restricted language λ, we reduce the semantic definition problem for L to that for λ. Such reduction may clear away a fair amount of superficial mess associated with L but absent in λ. Thus, for example, if we apply this method to FORTRAN we can eliminate the DO-statement from the FORTRAN language, replacing each DO-statement by an explicitly programmed iterative loop. Similarly, we could eliminate the calculated GO TO statement, reducing it to a block of IF-statements, etc. Applying this procedure systematically, we could re-express every FORTRAN program in terms of a considerably simplified subset of FORTRAN, and this might aid us considerably in giving a precise definition of the semantic significance of FORTRAN programs. As has been indicated, the method sketched here has been used wholeheartedly in defining the ALGOL 68 language. This language has at its center a core language whose semantics are carefully defined, basically in natural language. The core language is syntactically minimal; but a set of formal definitional mechanisms for extending it are given. To specify an extension, one describes the new syntactic forms which this extension is to embody, and for each such form, gives rules for the expression of the form in the base language. The ALGOL 68 language version intended for the normal user consists of the

base language, to which a standard definitional
preamble embodying the most useful extensions is
attached; the language user can in many cases by
adding other definitions work in a system especially
convenient for his particular application.

A third possible technique for semantic definition, and one that has certainly been proclaimed
often enough, is to define the semantics of a language by giving a compiler or interpreter for it.
However, interpreters are long, untransparent,
heavily involved with language-irrelevant machine
details, and always slightly unstable. Thus, in
employing an interpreter for definitional purposes
one wants to make use of a very special type of
interpreter, one which in contrast to the ordinary
case is maximally short, transparent, uninvolved
with machine-dependent details, and stable. The
process of defining a language may then still amount
to a type of programming, but programming of a very
special sort, possessing the virtues just mentioned,
but paying for them by foregoing efficient implemen-
tability. Using this technique, which was first
suggested by John McCarthy and which has since been
extended considerably in the ULD proposal emanating
from the IBM Vienna Laboratory, one defines a programming language L by first specifying, in mathematical terms, an abstract machine M. An interpreter for L written for M then constitutes the definition of L. Because of the abstractness of M, programming for it can be drastically simplified. For
example, since the memory of M is potentially
infinite, no space allocation problems arise; since
the speed of M is potentially infinite, implicit
searches may be used freely, etc. These facts permit
an interpreter written for M to be considerably
simpler than an interpreter written with more
attention to those questions of efficiency which so
dominate ordinary programming. Condensation brings
transparency and stability as corollary benefits.

It may profitably be remarked that the approach
described here has general applicability to the
process of algorithmic specification, and is not
limited merely to use in the definition of languages.

Mathematics itself may be regarded as that which
programming becomes when freed of all considerations
of efficiency; whereby infinite sets, implicit
definitions, transfinite functions, etc., become
permissible. A half step in this direction, that
is, a programming language which is still in principle implementable but in which considerations of
efficiency are largely hidden or suppressed, can
allow succinctness of expression to an unusual
degree. Let me remark that I see only two general
ways for a language to attain great expressive
power, and the method just described, which may be
called *mathematization* of the language, i.e., its
abstraction from considerations of efficiency, is
one of them. The other is the adaptation of the
language to a specific subject area, i.e., the
incorporation into the language of constructions and
dictions particularly useful to a given area. In
this sense, for example, FORTRAN is particularly apt
for array calculations, SNOBOL for work with strings,
etc. LISP gains some of its power by incorporating
structures (lists) particularly useful for work with
symbolic entities, but perhaps gains more through
mathematization, which in LISP takes the form of a
systematic commitment to the use of recursion, a
style of programming in which considerations of
efficiency are to a certain extent suppressed. These
reflections suggest a criterion which those attend-
ing the present symposium may profitably apply to
any semantic definition method presented in talks to
follow: to what extent does this method embody
devices specifically useful for semantics; to what
extent does its power rest upon such general mathematical grounds as the use of recursion, implicit
modes of expression, and general set-theoretic
dictions? On the syntactic side of the language
definition problem we may claim to have discovered
devices particularly useful to the subject to be
treated, namely those notions of sentence generation
from formal grammars which are embodied in the
various versions of the Backus metalanguage. In
semantics, concepts of a like simplifying power seem
to me not to be known, and hence in my opinion the
expressive power of semantic definition languages
rests rather directly on the general set-theoretical

principles which they embody, that is, on their
mathematization.

This concludes my general remarks on the semantic definition problem, and I now turn to my final
topic, and anticipation of certain directions of
language development likely to be of future importance.

I propose in this connection a classification
of programming languages into two major subcategor-
ies: *Computational languages* and *Object-describing
languages,* which might also be called *Languages of
mechanism.* Computational languages serve to describe the combination of functions, either by
simple combination, by iterative combination, or by
recursive combination. Most present programming
languages, e.g., FORTRAN, ALGOL 68, APL, LISP,
and PL/1, are of this general type. Languages of
mechanism, which are in a certain sense of higher
level than computational languages, serve not to
combine functions but to define functions which
can then be used in computational languages. In a
computational language we describe algorithms; in
a language of mechanism we describe objects, to
which algorithms determined by their form and yielding function values determined by the parameters of
an object are understood to apply. The relatively
few existing languages which can be regarded as
tending toward the type of languages of mechanism
(SNOBOL, certain metalanguages, one or two simulation languages, and certain languages developed in
connection with engineering applications) have not
been realized in ways which make their novel semantic character particularly plain. But I wish to
suggest that languages of this kind will play an
increasingly important future role. For this
reason, a simple language of mechanism will be
outlined in the following paragraphs, and its
semantic character contrasted with that of the more
familiar class of computational languages. In order,
however, that this contrast shall emerge sharply, I
first survey the more familiar class of computational
languages.

As has been stated, computational languages
serve to describe the simple, iterative, and recursive combination of functions. Computational languages may be classified according to the complexity
of the objects and basic functions which they
provide.

The simplest computational languages are the
machine-level assembly languages. A language of
this type provides only rudimentary data types
(machine words) and a limited, fixed repertoire of
functions (essentially the wired instructions of a
particular machine). Function combination is
expressed only by succession of operations; iteration
only by explicitly written transfers; and recursion
not at all.

At the next level of sophistication among computational languages we find such languages as
FORTRAN. Languages of this kind provide a few data
types (integers, reals, dimensional arrays); provide
certain basic operations related to these data types
(notably indexed access operations for dealing with
arrays); and allow the combination of functions in
considerably more convenient ways (function nesting,
infix operations) than are allowed by assembly
languages. Iteration forms represented by special
DO- and FOR-statements and recursion may also be
provided. Languages of this kind may quite naturally
be extended to include a greater variety of data
objects and of corresponding basic operations; such
extensions are made by PL/1 and various other languages which provide methods for data structuring
more general than array dimensioning.

A still more sophisticated or specialized computational language will refer directly to compound
objects and will provide operators dealing directly
with such objects. Examples are LISP, which uses
binary lists; APL, which works with arrays as
objects; and more explicitly set-theoretical languages which may be defined without undue difficulty.
ALGOL 68, another interesting member of this same
general subclass of computational languages, includes
mechanisms allowing the definition of structured node

types of variable layout and allows the dynamic
creation, within a growing structure, of nodes of any
described kind; since nodes may contain pointers to
other nodes, compound data items can be built up
in a rather general way out of networks of nodes.
ALGOL 68 systematically maintains awareness of the
type of each node which it is called upon to process,
and thereby enables its users to define operators
in an operand-type dependent manner.

All of the languages mentioned thus far are
computational, in that they are concerned with
functions and their algorithmic combination. Languages of mechanism by contrast serve not for the
combination but for the definition of functions.
In a language of mechanism, one deals not with
procedures but with *mechanisms* or *models*. With
each fully described model certain functions will
be associated; by using a language of mechanism to
define a model one is able to specify these functions
in an effective way. A model is described by list-
ing its *parts* and describing the *connections* of
these parts. To define a part within a language of
mechanism, one specifies the manner in which the
part reacts to all other parts to which it is
connected; these specifications, together with a
description of the interconnection pattern characterizing a given mechanism, will determine the action
of the mechanism, i.e., will determine certain
mechanism-related functions. Among languages of
mechanism, we may envision *discrete* languages, which
serve for the description of models whose parts pass
in discrete time periods between discrete states,
and *continuous* languages which serve for the description of models the states of those parts are defined
by continuous parameters varying by infinitesimal
degrees. For these languages we may distinguish
between *dynamic* models, the variation of whose state
in time is to be followed, and *static* models, which
serve to describe some physical or statistical
equilibrium. Among existing languages of mechanism
we may note the engineering language STRESS, which
in the above terms would be classified as a continuous static language, and certain simulation languages, notably GPSS, which may be described as

discrete dynamic languages. We may also admit as a
subclass the languages of *pattern*, in which a fixed
algorithm is applied to a variety of abstract objects
serving as patterns, thereby allowing one to define
useful functions; SNOBOL, as well as various syntactic metalanguages, belong to this class. However,
existing languages exemplify the general notion of
a language of mechanism only imperfectly. I shall
now sketch a hypothetical language of mechanism in
which the general nature of such languages will hopefully emerge more clearly. This will be a continuous
static language, intended for the description of
linear systems, which, in order that it have a name,
I shall call LINL. LINL, as any language of mechanism, will include statements allowing the description of *parts* of large assemblies, of *subassemblies*
of complete assemblies, and of *interconnections*
between parts. The complete LINL definition of an
assembly (i.e., mechanism or model) will determine
various model-related functions; LINL will include
linguistic devices for the specification of particular model-related functions whose values may be
required, and for the linkage of LINL to a computa-
tional-level language in which appropriate values
of these functions may be used.

A part-type eventually to be incorporated into
a larger assembly is defined in LINL by a *partype*
block. Such a block consists of a *header* line,
followed by a set of *equations*, and terminated by
the key word *end*. Each LINL line is punctuated by
a terminating semicolon. A partype header line has
the following appearance:

(1)   partype name (pname1, pname2, ...,
pnamek); Here *partype* is a key word; *name* may be
any valid name, which by virtue of its occurrence
in (1) is declared as the name of a part-type, while
pname1, ..., *pnamek* are the names of the *external
parameters* of the part-type declared in (1), and
play a special role to be outlined in more detail
in what follows. The following is an example of a
header line:

        partype resistor (v1, i1, v2, i2);

After its header line, the remainder of a partype
block consists of a set of equations separated by
semicolons. Each of these equations has the form

(2)   expression1 = expression2;

where each of the expressions occurring has a real
or complex number as its value. In (2) both
expression1 and *expression2* are required to have the
form

(3) $C_0 + C_1 *$pname1$+ C_2 *$pname2$+ ... + C_k *$pnamek

where *pname1,...,pnamek* are the external parameters
declared in the header of the partype block in which
(3) occurs, and where the coefficients

$$C_0, C_1, ..., C_k$$

may be arbitrary expressions containing various other
complex, real, integer, boolean, etc., parameters,
which we shall call the *internal parameters* of the
part-type. The following simple partype block will
illustrate the manner in which equations are to
occur:

partype resistor (v1, i1, v2, i2); v1-v2=res*i2;
          i1 +i2 = 0; end;

This block defines a type of part which might occur
within a larger (electrical) model, namely a resistor with two points of connection ("ends"), the
first held at the voltage v1 and with the emerging
current i1; the second held at the voltage v2 and
with the emerging current i2. Note that the first
of the two equations stated above expresses Ohm's
law, while the second of these equations expresses
the conservation of charge. The parameter *res* which
occurs in the partype block shown above is an internal parameter of the part-type defined by this block,
namely the ohmic resistance of a resistor.

    Once part-types and their associated equations
have been defined in LINL, parts of the various
defined types may be used to build up composite

subassemblies and complete models. To define a subassembly one uses a *subassembly block* consisting of
a *header line,* of a *parts enumeration,* and of a set
of *connection statements,* the whole terminated by
an *end* statement. The header line of a subassembly
block has the form

    (4)   assemble name (pname1, pname2, ..., pnamek)

Here, *assemble* is a keyword; *name* may be any valid
name, which by virtue of its occurrence in (4) is
declared as the name of a subassembly type; while
pname1,...,pnamek, are the names of the external
parameters of the subassembly declared with the
header line (4); the special role which these external parameters play will be outlined in more detail
in what follows. To illustrate the use of such a
subassembly header line, note that a LINL description of a four-terminal electrical subassembly
having the form shown schematically in Figure 1
below might begin with the following header line

    assemble module (v1, i1, v2, i2, v3, i3, v4, i4);

Figure 1

A Hypothetical Four-Terminal Subassembly

Here, v1, v2, v3, and v4 designate the voltages at
which the four connection points to be the subassembly
shown in Figure 1 will be held, while i1, i2, i3,
and i4 designate the currents emerging from these
four points.

After the header line of a subassembly block there follows the parts enumeration of the block. This statement has the form

use partspecl, partspec2, ..., partspecm;

in which *use* is a keyword, and each of the *parts specification clauses* which follows this keyword has the form

(5)   typename (partnamel, partname2, ...,
           partnamek).

If, for example, the four-terminal subassembly abstract that represents it in Figure 1 has the more detailed form shown in Figure 2, its parts might be enumerated as follows:

use resistor (rl, r2, r3, r4)

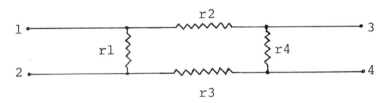

Figure 2

A Particular Four-Terminal Subassembly

As this example illustrates, *typename* in (5) must be the name of a previously declared part-type or subassembly. Moreover, still in (5), each of *partnamel,...,partnamek* will be either a *simple name* or an *indexed name range*, designating in any case an elementary part of a particular subassembly out of which a more comprehensive subassembly is to be constructed. Any valid name may serve as a simple name. An indexed name range will have the form

(6)   name (indexname ε set-expression).

An example of this type of construction is

$$\gamma(k\epsilon\{1,2,3,4\}),$$

in terms of which we might, for example, describe the parts of the four-terminal subassembly shown in Figure 2 by the statement

use resistor (r(k$\epsilon\{1,2,3,4\}$)).

After the header line and the parts enumeration of a subassembly there follow several successive connection statements. Connection statements may be either *simple* or *repetitive*. A simple connection statement has one of the two forms

(7)   ident datspec1, datspec2, ..., datspecn;

and

(8)   ztotal datspec1, datspec2, ..., datspecn;

The data specifications *datspec1,...,datspecn* occurring in (7) and (8) will either be *qualified names*, or will be *qualified name sets*. A qualified name has the form

paramname . objectname.

Here *objectname* is the name of an object 0 which is to form part of an assembly being described; this name must have occurred in a preceding *use* statement. Moreover, *paramname* is the name of an external para-meter belonging to objects of the type 0; this name must have occurred either in a preceding *partype* statement or in a preceding *assemble* statement. The combination *paramname . objectname* then designates a particular parameter of a particular object and hence represents a particular numerical parameter of the total model to be described.

A qualified name set has the form

(9) paramname . name (indexname ϵ
                        set-expression).

Here an indexed set of objects, all of the same type, occurs; this set must form part of an indexed set of objects declared in some preceding *use* statement. Moreover, *paramname* is the name of an external parameter belonging to objects of this type, and must have been declared previously in a partype or an assemble statement. The combination (9) then designates a particular set of parameters of a particular set of objects, and hence represents a particular set of numerical parameters of the total model to be described.

If all the data specifications occurring in (7) are simple names, then (7) has the same logical force as the family of equations

(10) datspec1 = datspec2 = ... = datspecn;.

Similarly, if all the data specifications occurring in (8) are simple names, then (8) is equivalent in logical force to the single equation

(11) datspec1 + datspec2 + ... + datspecn = 0.

The manner in which an indexed name set occurring within a connection statement is to be interpreted can best be explained by a few examples. The connection statement

ident v.rr, v.r (jε{1,2,3,4})

is equivalent in logical force to the set of equations

v.rr = v.r(1) = v.r(2) = ... = v.r(4);

the connection statement

ztotal v.rr, v.r (jε{1,2,3,4})

is equivalent in logical force to the single equation

v.rr + v.r(1) + v.r(2) = v.r(4) = 0.

A repetitive connection statement has one of the two forms

(12) $(vk_1 \ \varepsilon \ setexp1, \ vk_2 \ \varepsilon \ setexp2(k_1), \ vk_3 \ \varepsilon$
setexp3$(k_1,k_2) \ ...)$ (ident datspec1, ...,
datspecn);

(13) $(vk_1 \ \varepsilon \ setexp1, \ vk_2 \ \varepsilon \ setexp2(k_1),$
$vk_3 \ \varepsilon \ setexp3 \ (k_1,k_2)...)$
(ztotal datspec1, ..., datspecn).

In LINL, a total model is described by a sub-assembly block in which no external parameters are declared. Once a complete model has been described in LINL, it is treated as follows. A complete list of all its parts and of all external parameters of these parts is generated. All the (possibly inhomogeneous) linear equations satisfied by these parameters, both those given within the partype blocks defining particular types of parts, and those given within connection statements occurring in subassembly blocks are collected. The availability of as many equations as parameters and the occurrence of each parameter in at least one equation is verified, and suitable diagnostics issued if this verification fails. Code suitable for the calculation of each external parameter of every part and subassembly using this family of linear equations is generated. Any code required for the calculation of any coefficient function C_j occurring in the explicit form of an expression constituting part of an equation (3) is also generated. The total code obtained will calculate every external parameter of each part of a total model once all the internal parameters of the model have been established.

In a later paragraph, we will describe several straightforward linguistic mechanisms which allow the parameters of a model described in LINL to be referenced from within a language of computational level; this linkage once established, LINL models may be used to define functions for use in a computational language, which functions may be evaluated, used within more expensive computations, perhaps for purposes of optimization, etc.

Before describing these linkages between LINL and a language of computational level, however, we prefer to give a more explicit illustration of the use of LINL. To this end, we shall outline the way in which LINL may be used to describe an electrical filter network having the form shown schematically in Figure 3.

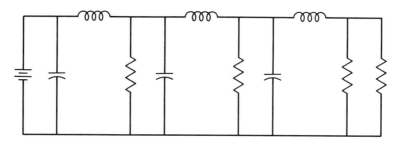

Figure 3

A Filter Network with Power Source
And Load Resistor

The basic components of the network shown in Figure 3 may be declared as follows:

```
partype resistor(vl, il, v2, i2);
  v2-vl = res*i2; il + i2 = 0; end;

partype choke(vl, il, v2, i2);
  vl-v2 = m*f*il; il + i2 = 0; end;

partype cap(vl, il, v2, i2);
  vl-v2 = (c/f)*il; il + i2 = 0; end;

partype vsource(vl, il, v2, i2);
  vl = 0; v2 = v; il + i2 = 0; end;
```

It is plainly convenient in describing the net-work shown in Figure 3 to make use of the four-input subassembly shown in Figure 4. This subassembly may be described as follows in LINL:

```
assemble stage(vl, il, v2, i2, v3, i3, v4, i4);
use choke(a), cap(c), resistor(r);
ident vl, v2.c, vl.a;
ztotal il, i2.c; il.a;
ident v3, v2.a, vl.r;
ztotal i3, i2.a, il.r;
ident v2, il.c, v2.r,v4;
ztotal i2, il.c, i2.r, i4; end;
```

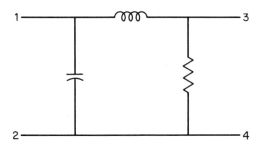

Figure 4

Simple Stage in a Filter Network

Using subassemblies of this kind, we may describe the total network shown in Figure 3 as follows:

```
assemble network;
use vsource(vs), resistor(load), stage
              stage s(j∈{1,2,3});
ident. vl.vs, vl.s(1);
ident v2.vs, v2.s(1);
ztotal il.vs, il.s(1)
ztotal i2.vs, i2.s(1);
(∀j∈{1,2})(ident v3.s(j), vl.s(j+1) );
(∀j∈{1,2})(ztotal i3.s(j), il.s(j+1) );
(∀j∈{1,2})(ident v4.s(j), v2.s(j+1) );
(∀j∈{1,2})(ztotal i4.s(j), i2.s(j+1) );
ident v3.s(3), vl.load;
ident v4.s(3), vl.load;
ztotal i3.s(3), il.load;
ztotal i4.s(3), i2.load; end;
```

This provides a sufficiently extensive illustration of the use of LINL to describe a total model and we now turn to discuss the manner in which LINL may be linked to a language of computational level within which functions associated with models described in LINL can be used. Note, to begin with, that the collection of parts constituting a total LINL model has a structure determined by the details of the model description. More specifically, each part of a subassembly has a name defined by the use statement in which it is declared. Each sub-part of a larger subassembly has in the same way a specific name, and each part in a total LINL model may be referred to unambiguously by a unique chain of subassembly names. Thus, for example, in the network model just described, the part represented by the middle vertical line of Figure 3 can be referenced by the string

    r.s(2)

and the external parameters of this part may then be referenced by name strings such as

    v1.r.s(2), v2.r.s(2), etc;

the internal parameters of the same part may be referenced in very similar fashion as

    res.r.s(2), etc.

We might incorporate this straightforward observation in a formal linguistic mechanism as follows: within a procedural language (think for specificity of PL/1, or for that matter of FORTRAN) special *linkage subroutines* which connect the procedural language to LINL are to be provided. These linkage subroutines may have some such form as the following: a header line, having much the same form as a normal procedure-block declaration header could introduce a linkage subroutine; an "end" statement in whatever form the procedural language finds convenient could terminate the subroutine. The internal test of the subroutine would specify some particular LINL assembly, and would also include a

collection of equivalence declarations identifying
all the internal parameters of the assembly, and
certain of its external parameters, with the formal
parameters of the linkage subroutine. This internal
test should also include supplementary declarations
which designate certain of the formal parameters of
the linkage subroutine as input parameters, while
other parameters are designated as output parameters.

The linkage thus established would then make
the parameters of the LINL model accessible within
the procedural language, enabling certain of these
parameters to be "set" and the values of others to
be "read." The LINL compiler would then check that
enough input information to permit the calculation
of all the output parameters had been supplied,
issuing appropriate diagnostics if this check failed,
and setting up the code for the necessary calculations if the check was successful. All in all, LINL
would function as a function-defining supplement to
the procedural language. While it is true that all
the equations which the LINL compiler supplies could
also be set up by hand by a skilled programmer
working directly from the circuit model declared
within LINL, such a procedure would of course be
far less convenient; the typical situation in which
a language and a compiler prove themselves useful.

The example which we have just considered at
length illustrates the general point that a programming language, if it is not merely to be a syntactic
format within which certain standard services can
be invoked, must embody some interesting and useful
"algebra" of complex objects and parameters, as well
as a specialized notation system for representing
these objects and parameters, and the operations
associated with them. I say here "algebra" since,
unless the objects with which one is dealing can be
iteratively combined to build up objects of potentially unbounded complexity, one may in fact have
what amounts only to a mechanism for invoking a
fixed, even if large, collection of pre-programmed
services. The following short catalog (which
indicates the wide range of possibilities for the
construction of such algebras) will illustrate this

point. We can build algebras around

1. Arrays and their various combinations and transformations.
      Example: APL.
2. Lists, and their recursive evaluation.
      Example: LISP.
3. Sets, maps, and their various combinations.
      Example: SETL.
4. Strings, patterns, and the matching operations
which relate them.
      Example: SNOBOL.
5. Electric circuits and their interconnections.
      Examples: LINL, and other similar electrical
                 engineering languages.
6. General classes of objects interacting through
discrete events.
      Examples: SIMSCRIPT, SIMULA, GPSS, and various
                 other discrete simulation languages.
7. Algebraic formulae, and their various manipu-
lations.
      Examples: FORMULA ALGOL, MATHLAB, and other
                 languages for algebraic manipula-
                 tions.
8. Elastic structures formed out of thin members,
and their interconnections.
      Examples: STRESS, COGO, and various other
                 mechanical engineering languages.
9. Generative Grammars, syntactic types and their
subgrammars, and strings.
      Examples: various language-describing meta-
                 languages.
10. Plane or three-dimensional figures, and their
geometric combinations and relations.
      Examples: various languages for figure-pro-
                 duction and analysis.

Consideration of these examples suggests a
tentative answer to the question "What are programming languages?"; a question evidently fateful for
all future efforts to design semantic specification
tools. The answer suggested is as follows:

Programming languages are notational systems

devised to facilitate the description of abstract
objects whose basic elements are sets, mappings,
and processes. With these objects there is to be
associated a well-defined rule for evaluating them;
perhaps, since the objects may contain processes as
subparts, it would be better to say, for interpreting them. From this point of view, an imperative
programming language of the ordinary serial kind
may be regarded as a mechanism for the description
of a set of basic blocks, with each of which is
associated a family of possible successors. Each
block must also be furnished with a "terminating
conditional transfer" which can be used during
interpretation of the program to select one poten-
tial successor block as the actual "point of transfer." This familiar kind of location-counter
control is, however, only one of the many quite
different possibilities which are illustrated by the
languages listed above. In simulation languages,
for example, the basic principle of organization is
different: the subprocesses of a simulation naturally form an unordered set, each of which is furnished with an invocation condition. The simulation
interpreter executes, in any order, all processes
whose invocation condition is satisfied, as long as
any remain to be executed; when none remain, an
underlying time-parameter is advanced by the interpreter, and the next cycle of simulation begins.

If we bear in mind this broad range of possibilities, the following point of view suggests itself. The "front" or "syntactic" part of a language
system must provide methods by means of which very
general abstract objects (graph-like, rather than
tree-like, i.e., admitting remote rather than purely
local connections) can be described conveniently.
This "front end" should be variable enough so that
the descriptive notation to be used can be tailored
to the requirements of any particular field,
permitting the objects of most common concern in
this field to be described in a succinct and
heuristically comfortable manner. Powerful mechanisms for describing the diagnostic or verification
tests to be applied to text during its syntactic
analysis should also form part of this language-

system front end. The "back" or interpreter part of
a language system should incorporate abstract structures which are general enough so that whatever
structured objects may be of concern in any conceiv-
able situation can conveniently be mapped upon these
structures.

The use of general set theory should certainly
satisfy this latter requirement, as long as the
actual use of theorem-proving methods is not at
issue. Set theory could only fail to be adequate
if some other entities than sets were directly
accessible to mathematical intuition and could therefore be used as a fundamental starting point independent of set theory, which is not the case. Thus,
if a suitably flexible syntactic front end were
attached to a set-theoretic language we would have
a system covering a good part of all that is likely
to be found along that road which completely by-
passes considerations of efficiency. Of course,
this would still leave room for semi-general languages which compromise artfully with full generality
in order to reach higher efficiencies than would
otherwise be attainable.

Beyond the procedural languages we expect the
development of languages of mechanism to begin, and
hope that this paper has illuminated some of the
forces which will influence such a development.

FORMAL SEMANTIC DEFINITION USING SYNTHESIZED AND INHERITED ATTRIBUTES

Wayne T. Wilner
Stanford University

The work which follows is essentially a sequel to that presented by Donald Knuth in his 1968 paper "Semantics of Context-Free Languages" [2].

The basic idea is to formalize semantics by giving meaning to the terminal and non-terminal symbols in a context-free grammar. Then the meaning of any string in the language is the combined meanings of all the symbols in a parse tree for the string. Knuth's essential idea is to express the meaning of each symbol solely in terms of the meanings of its immediate neighbors in a parse tree. This restriction leads to definitions which can be made brief without jeopardizing comprehensibility, and intuitive without sacrificing machine-readability.

We can use a context-free grammar for binary notation to remind everyone of the details and to illustrate these claims. This grammar contains a set of productions:

(1)	$B \to 0$
(2)	$B \to 1$
(3)	$L \to B$
(4)	$L_1 \to L_2\ B$
(5)	$F \to B$
(6)	$F_1 \to B\ F_2$
(7)	$N \to L$
(8)	$N \to L\ .\ F;$

a start symbol, $S = N$; a set of non-terminal symbols
$\{B,L,F,N\}$; and a set of terminal symbols $\{0,1\}$
(subscripts are used only to distinguish between
occurrences of like non-terminals). For any string
on this language, this grammar generates a parse
tree: e.g. "101.01"

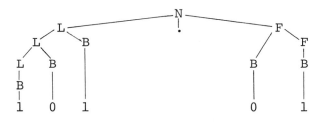

There may be more than one parse tree, each having
its own meaning. Having this grammar we now simply
say that a string in binary notation represents a
real number, which we already understand. More
precisely, any sequence of binary digits $b_k b_{k-1} \ldots b_0$
stands for the sum of various powers of two; namely

$$b_k b_{k-1} \ldots b_0 = b_k * 2^k + b_{k-1} * 2^{k-1} + \ldots + b_0 * 2^0 .$$

This expression makes use of all the concepts we
need to explicate any binary number; so let us add
the symbols we have used to our grammar. In addition to terminal and non-terminal symbols for syntax,
we now have terminal (and later, non-terminal)
symbols for semantics. In this case, they are the
terminal semantic symbol set

$C = \{ * , 2 , 0 , 1 , + , - , \{Real\ numbers\},$
        $exponentiation\}$

The vehicles by which we attach meaning to non-terminal symbols are what Knuth and others have called *attributes*, functions whose values are derived from our basic concepts. Each non-terminal symbol has a number of attributes; what they are exactly depends on who is specifying the semantics. This is why we can write "intuitive" semantic specifications; there is a great deal of freedom in choosing attributes. For example, we may feel that it is acceptable to say that binary digits, B, binary numbers, N, and their syntactic parts, L and F, possess values, so we will let *value* be the name of one attribute. In addition, we have been taught in school that digits have place values, so we will let that be an attribute which we will call *scale*. These names constitute our non-terminal semantic vocabulary, and are added to our grammar as a set named A, for attributes.

It is Knuth's suggestion that the functions which specify these attributes be expressible in terms of attribute values of immediate neighbors in the parse tree. What we mean by *immediate neighbors* are those symbols which appear together in a single production. In other words, we define attribute functions on a rule-by-rule basis. The meaning of a whole program is thus constructed only out of local meanings. Applying this to our example, we augment each rule as follows:

(1) $B \rightarrow 0$; $V_B = 0 * 2^S B = 0$

    This says that the value associated with a zero bit is zero.

(2) $B \rightarrow 1$; $V_B = 1 * 2^S B = 2^S B$

    This says that the value associated with a one bit is whatever power of two corresponds to the bit's position.

(3) $L \rightarrow B$; $V_L = V_B$; $S_B = S_L$

(4) $L_1 \rightarrow L_2 B$; $V_{L1} = V_{L2} + V_B$; $S_{L2} = S_{L1} + 1$; $S_B = S_{L1}$

This expresses the notion we saw earlier,
that the value of a string of binary digits
is the sum of the values of each digit.
The second function, for S_{L2}, says that
the position of the list of bits L_2 is one
greater than what we thought it was.

(5) $F \rightarrow B;$ $V_F = V_B;$ $S_B = S_F$

(6) $F_1 \rightarrow BF_2;$ $V_{F1} = V_{B2} + V_{F2};$ $S_{F2} = S_{F1} - 1;$ $S_B = S_{F1}$

Likewise, the positions of the bits F_2 are
reckoned to be one less than that of bit B.

(7) $N \rightarrow L$ $S_1 = 0;$ $V_N = V_L$

(8) $N \rightarrow L.F;$ $S_L = 0;$ $S_F = -1;$ $V_N = V_L + V_F$

Productions 7 and 8 give initial conditions
for the scale attribute. They also define
functions for the most significant attribute,
V_N, the value of the entire number.

This forms a new set of productions, P', which now,
supposedly, contains all the semantic and syntactic
information that we need in order to understand
strings in the language.

To see how these attributes look in a derivation
tree, let us complete our sample tree (see next
page).

I write the value attribute on the bottom side
of non-terminals because it depends only on information lower down in the tree; that is, if we look
at a single production, the value attribute is
specified for the left-hand side symbol in terms of
attributes of right-hand side symbols — never the
other way around. This is called a *synthesized
attribute*. I write the scale attribute on the top
side of non-terminals because the reverse is true:
it is always specified for a right-hand side symbol,
usually in terms of the left. Thus it depends on

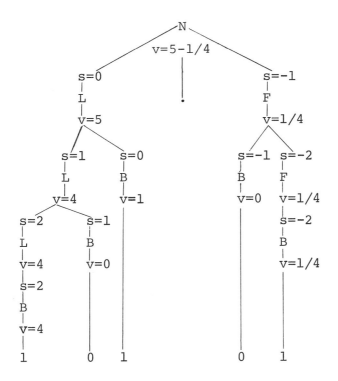

information higher in the tree, on context. This is called an *inherited attribute*.

In summary of Knuth's paper, we may say that we have expanded the definition of a context-free grammar by adding a semantic vocabulary and by postulating that each production has the form:

$$\# \; \alpha \rightarrow V^*; \; \{a = f\} \; \#$$

where "#" is the string delimiter, "α" is a syntactic non-terminal, "V^*" is a string of syntactic terminals and non-terminals, "{}" indicates a collection of things, "a" is a semantic non-terminal — either a synthesized attribute of α or an inherited attribute of some symbol in V^*, and f is a functional form whose arguments are semantic terminals and non-terminals — the non-terminals being restricted to

those which are possessed by syntactic non-terminals
which appear in the production. What this means is
that whenever a production is employed in the parse
tree of a string in the language, then its meaning
is given by the evaluation of the attribute functions
with their particular arguments. What we are doing
here is specifying a way in which information can
be passed up and down the parse tree of the language.

*Q: Can any specification for the way in which
information may be passed and transformed as it is
moved along the tree be reduced to the action of
attachment of a semantic function to each production
(possibly defining a non-terminal in the direction
of the information flow)?*

A: I don't know, but intuitively I'd have a hard
time constructing a counter-example.

   All right, how well did the theory perform in
its first big test? Let us begin by discussing
how to choose a semantic vocabulary suitable for
Simula 67, or a similar language. One must first
decide what one's purpose is in defining the language: it may be to explain the functional operation
of the various syntactic elements as in the program-
mers' manual; it may be to describe in a rigorous
way the machine code which a compiler is to produce;
it may be to relate strings in the language to some
mathematically appealing concepts, like recursive
functions; or it may simply be to express strings
in equivalent strings of another language. All of
these goals are compatible with the method. It is
up to the author of the semantic definition to
decide what his audience already understands and
would find convenient for defining a new language.

   When the time came to choose our primitive
ideas, we chose to relate Simula 67 to a Randall
and Russell-type opcode set. Actually, the people
supporting this research, Burroughs Corporation,
had been promised a Simula compiler, from me, so
that was a further stimulus for using machine
language as a semantic base.

Of course, I regard this choice as a cop-out;
we side-stepped the issue. All such a definition
really amounts to is a string-manipulating translator which does not confront the vital issues of
assignment and sequencing. So I think of my
definition as a training exercise for the real
battle, a second definition of Simula 67 in terms
of a more esthetically pleasing base.

Nevertheless, the definition of Simula 67
centers around an attribute which I unfortunately
called *rule*, meaning an operation rule. Its value
is a string of opcodes which, when executed, performs
the algorithm represented by the corresponding Simula
string. Let me illustrate this with the *S*imple
*A*rithmetic *E*xpression, the white rat of the computer
scientist. For the productions

(1)   SAE $\rightarrow$ T
(2)   SAE $\rightarrow$ AO T
(3) $SAE_1 \rightarrow SAE_2$ AO T
(4)   AO $\rightarrow$ +
(5)   AO $\rightarrow$ -
  .
  .
  .

if we translate into postfix polish form, rule 3
requires the attribute function

rule$[SAE_1]$ = rule$[SAE_2]$ rule[T] rule[AO] .

This says that the code for something like "A+B" is:
evaluate A, evaluate B, add the results. (Rule$[SAE_1]$
simply means the rule to be associated with SAE_1.)

Now notice something very interesting at rule
4. If we try to define the code for rule 4 by
itself, we are in trouble. We don't know if the
adding operator is unary or binary.

Well, there are several solutions. If we
forget that there are inherited attributes available to transmit contextual information, we might

assume the burden of omniscience and generate both unary and binary operations at rule 5.

rule[AO] - (SUB, NEG)

and select one later

rule[SAE_1] = rule[SAE_2] rule[T] (10)/rule[AO]

where that last term is an APL-like expression meaning "pick the first of two elements." A neater solution is to create an inherited boolean attribute *dyadic* which is an attribute of the addition operator. Then have it defined to be true in rule 3

SAE_1 → SAE_2 AO T; dyadic[AO] = true

and false in rule 2

SAE → AO T; dyadic[AO] = false

so that the function for rule in 5 can be

$$AO → - ; \text{rule}[AO] = \begin{matrix} \text{SUB, if dyadic[AO]} \\ \text{NEG, if } \sim \text{dyadic[AO]} \end{matrix}$$

Thus only the correct operation is synthesized.

This solution shows less interdependence among individual rules than the former in which we had to remember from one rule to the next which attributes were multi-valued and which were not. It is also less artificial; there are monadic and dyadic operators in real life, whereas I doubt if any compiler ever resolved the semantics of + and - by generating all possible instructions and later eliminating all but one.

Q: Could you not have a separate rule for unary operators that has the same right-hand side?

A: You could. That would solve the problem. But Simula does not. We have to work around the syntax.

Q: You wrote it that way?

A: I didn't write it that way. That is the ALGOL
report. I would be a lot happier if the syntax
was actually given in a form that would make the
specification of the semantics more natural, in
this case by having a separate rule for unary
operators.

When writing attribute functions for this rule,
there is some information you don't have now, thus
you must decide between alternative attribute values,
and this is in a sense semantically ambiguous.
Maybe we should say "equivocal." Equivocacy is
semantic ambiguity. Ambiguity is plain old syntactic
ambiguity.

This has illustrated the kind of information
that is best formulated by using inherited attributes.
They should bring a closer correspondence between
semantic rules and what you tell a programmer about
what is going on. For example, if you render rule
5 into English you might say: "one of the operator
symbols in Simula is a minus sign which can mean
either a subtraction or a negation, depending on
context." That must be about the shortest English
sentence you could use to describe the rule's semantics.

Perhaps this method is more of a contribution
to the art of technical writing than to formal
semantics.

Let me state a few figures. The Simula language has almost 400 syntax rules. We added 570
function definitions to these 400 rules to completely
describe the semantics. So it is about twice as
long as the syntax. There is a footnote to that —
you must describe the meaning of your basic concepts.
For Peter Lucas it is that long chapter where he
describes how the machine operates. We had to write
one like that too, but in the programming manual
context, it can usually be left out, since everyone
is supposed to understand the underlying machine.

In our first attempt to define Simula, we wrote
over 3000 rules. Somehow that did not strike us as

brief. We were able to find several reduction techniques which eliminated 80% of the rules. The information is still in the definition, it is just that 80% of the rules express redundant information. In its present form, our formal definition is shorter than the Simula language manual. Moreover, it also describes canonical compiler output for each language construct. So even though it is a few pages shorter, it is both more detailed and more unambiguous than the corresponding English description.

Let me emphasize that this is just a framework with which to express semantics, making no comments about semantics itself. If we take the set of concepts C to be simply the terminal symbols of ALGOL 68, and rewrite the productions of Simula 67, in those terms, when we are done we have described the translation of Simula 67 to ALGOL 68.

Perhaps we could reach for further semantic understanding by describing an interpreter in C. Then the meaning of a string in Simula 67 would be given in terms of the values that the program computes, rather than code to be executed later.

Q: Are you really saying that you could get out the value the program computes even if the program has loops?

A: Well, I seem to be out on a limb. If we are going to describe the actions of an interpreter in our semantic base it looks like this may break down. The point of this approach is to give a brief and comprehensible explanation of a programming language, and it is terrific as long as we stick to the typical situation of defining programming languages as manuals do. But if you are interested in more interesting semantic questions — and most of us are — then maybe this does not help. What it would be good for is a standard way to describe all the programming languages we use, hopefully opening the door to a little more insight into what differences and similarities there might be between these different languages.

*Q: When you use a program that gets into a loop,
what is your parser or whatever it is that uses this
going to do? Is it going to run on forever?*

A: I would imagine — if you have really been
successful at writing the semantics. I don't know.
I don't have any experience in this area.

*Q: Along the lines of that question, and to further
substantiate your feeling about difficulty realizing
interpreters, and also the difficulty of this method
for describing interpreters is an experience I've
had in using this method for the lambda calculus.*

*The problem was that having a parse of an
afferent expression, we might want to do a reduction
which may involve some renaming. We might want to
introduce a variable, not used elsewhere. In order
to do that, we have to pass this new variable that
we have introduced up the tree and back down through
the rest of the tree. After performing one reduction
we have to reparse so that the meaning of the root
node incorporated the naming of the lower node.
Thus, after we perform a reduction, we parse, and
continue until no further reductions were formed.
So, in the case of the program that did not terminate,
we would just keep on parsing. My feeling was that
there was another natural kind of attribute we might
want, which arose from the difficulty of passing a
newly created variable up and down the tree. It
would be some kind of global variable that all of
the nodes would have access to. In that way we
wouldn't have to keep reparsing. Granted, we realize
a global variable would keep changing, but we more
naturally think of some variables as being global.*

A: That is a good observation. There are some
semantic things which we think of as completely
global, yet this method insists you deal with one
production at a time, so we had to describe the
transmission of this information at every stage;
I don't honestly know which way is best. When Knuth
wrote his paper, he had global attributes. When I
did Simula 67, I found that they could all come out
so that every rule is in fact isolated. Each way

takes the same amount of effort, for Algol-like languages. Perhaps the lambda calculus is different.

*Q: Was it possible to put the global variables into
this technique however inefficiently? (Addressed
to McGowen)*

A: Well, we did it this way: when we did rename,
we would pass back the name as an attribute to all
the other nodes that might need it. If we could
form a second computation after a second parse, then
we again passed that as an attribute. Also, when
we selected our new variable, among the attributes
available at the time was a list of variables appearing elsewhere. I think if this is taken in full
generality you have trees being attributes of the
nodes.

WILNER: Right... that is one of the more intriguing
things, the admission of tree attributes in general.
If you think about Simula and the code you might
generate for it, you would really want to generate
the execution tree that Peter Lucas described —
that would be the most natural. And so what you
would end up with at the top node is a whole new
tree of the program, but one that would execute
instead of just parse it.

*Q: I have a hunch that there is going to be a paper
written in which something like the notion of
deterministic grammar is applied to the semantic
rules in this form. I suspect that the components
of whatever it is that passes for determinants —
it isn't going to be left or right anymore — is
not going to be the issue. I think there are going
to be two issues: the first is the idea of visiting
each node once somehow in the process of evaluating
the semantic function — or perhaps twice, once
down and then up; and the second one is the idea that
the information that is passed can not begin to
explode so that it has become increasingly more
difficult to deal with each node, as would happen
if for example you had concatenation as one of the
functions.*

*Q: In your definition of Simula, did you have to
go through a computer program to check that there
were no circularly defined attributes?*

A: Not really. Let me first mention that Knuth
has a new algorithm for circularity. There is a
mistake in the one he published (his corrections to
his original paper, including a correct algorithm,
will appear in Volume 4 or 5 of *Mathematical Systems
Theory*). There was only one occasion when I came
close to writing a function that was obviously
circular. It had to do with class declarations.
There is an attribute called environment — it is
uncanny how Peter Lucas and I use the same names —
which amounts to a symbol table. Naturally, you
write the semantics of statements assuming the
symbol table is complete. But in class and procedure
declarations, whose semantics have to do with com-
pleting the symbol table, there are those trouble-
some statements, appearing prematurely, so to speak.
So it looks as though you have to have the symbol
table all filled in before you can finish filling
it in. Well, after you think about it, you realize
that it is only the class heading you need, not
the statements in its body, so there is no real
circularity. It never quite takes place. So I never
showed that the Simula definition was not circular
because the answer was so obviously no.

     Incidentally, I should mention that Knuth's
next student, Isu Fang, is going to implement a
general program that will accept a 6-tuple and output a program that will accept any string and convert
it into its equivalent tree with its attribute values
filled in.

*Q: To accept a 6-tuple you have to have some way of
accepting C?*

A: Well, this is the old problem that all compiler-
compilers have had, anticipating different semantics.
Nearly all of Simula's attribute functions, though,
are simply one of four functions: either a constant
function, or identity, or addition, or subtraction.
This is about all we really use. So it may not be

impossible.

Q: Do you put any restrictions on kinds of semantic rules?

A: That would be the next interesting thing to do. Certainly, if you are going to make them machine readable, the easiest way is to impose restrictions, but that defeats the real purpose of allowing an intuitive description. Fang really has his work cut out for him here! I don't know how he is going to manage it, but I imagine it will use the same compromise that the compiler-compilers have used — make assumptions and force people to live with them.

Q: Is your description of Simula 67 available?

A: It is now a disc file in Paoli, Pennsylvania. But I guess it will be in the library probably by December, because we are ready to do the final typing.

Q: Will you give us the source? (laughter)

Q: You said that Knuth's algorithm for detecting circularity was wrong. Did he know where it is wrong?

A: No, he did not elaborate. It is surprisingly hard to find such an algorithm, and that means it is hard to understand it and hard to find out what is wrong.

REFERENCES

[1] Foundation Work

Irons, E.T., "Towards More Versatile Mechanical Translators," *American Mathematical Society Symposium on Applied Mathematics*, Vol 15, p. 41-50.

[2]   Preceeding Work

Knuth, D.E., "Semantics of Context-Free Languages," *Mathematical Systems Theory*, Vol. 2
No. 2, 1968, p. 127-145

[3]   Succeeding Work

————, "Examples of Formal Semantics," *Computer
Science Report No.169*, Computer Science
Department, Stanford University.

Wilner, W.T., "A Declarative Semantic Definition," *Ph.D. Thesis*, 1971, Computer Science
Department, Stanford University.

[4]   Contrasting Work

Weber, H., Wirth, N., "Euler; A Generalization
of Algol and Its Formal Definition," *Communica-
tions of the ACM*, 1966, Vol. 9, No. 1,2,
p. 11-25, 89-99, 878.

PL/I Definition Group of the Vienna Laboratory,
Formal Definition of PL/I, IBM Technical Report
TR 25.071, 1966.

ON
THE SEMANTICS
OF
PROGRAMMING LANGUAGES
AND
SOFTWARE
DEVICES

Peter Lucas
IBM Laboratory Vienna

A history of the ideas and motivations of the contributions of the IBM Vienna Laboratory to the subject of formal semantics of programming languages is presented. Recent investigations and future plans concerning the formalization of implementation techniques are discussed.

INTRODUCTION

The contribution of the Vienna Laboratory to the subject of formal semantics of programming languages has been presented on several occasions in considerable technical detail [11].

I do not want to go over these details again. Instead it seems appropriate, at this point in time, to present first a history of ideas and motivations together with some critical remarks. The second part of my talk will be concerned with recent investigations on the formalization of implementation techniques and future plans.

Part of the paper assumes familiarity with [11].

HISTORY OF IDEAS AND MOTIVATIONS

The early activity on formal language definition
at the Vienna Laboratory started as a result of our
experience with implementations of ALGOL 60. It was
felt that the design of a correct implementation
constitutes a nontrivial problem and that therefore
a more precise definition on a formal basis was
desirable. Early attempts were based upon a BNF
syntax definition and aimed at a semantic description
of complicated language constructs in terms of primitive ones (H. Bekic [1]). In the later stage of
the development, primarily through the influence of
publications by J. McCarthy [12], we accepted the
idea of an *abstract syntax* as the basis plus a direct
interpretation of the language constructs instead of
a reduction to a primitive core language. It should
be mentioned that the introduction of an abstract
syntax greatly facilitated the task of defining a
large language like PL/1. In fact it is frightening
to think of the complications and size of the definition, if we had based the PL/1 definition directly
upon a BNF syntax.

The basic principle of the definition method
hardly needs any comment. The main constituents of
a programming language are commands. In order to
describe the meaning of a command one ought to
describe, in some way or another, for all possible
states of the considered system, what state of the
system is established after the command is executed.
The description of all machine languages I know of
follows this pattern. One way to mathematically
describe a command is by a function mapping states
into states [6].

The first proposal I know of which makes it
explicit that the same principle ought to be applied
to higher-level languages was made by J. McCarthy
[12] and presented in depth at a WG 2.1 meeting in
Delft, 1963. On this occasion J. McCarthy also
introduced the concept of an abstract syntax.

As indicated in the following history, it was a
long and painful path which led from the basic

principles to the actual specification of an appropriate abstract machine which reflects the properties of PL/1.

The project to produce a formal and complete
definition of PL/1 started in October 1965 and was
carried out in close cooperation with the IBM
Hursley Laboratories.

By the time the project started we had more
or less settled on the definition method to be used,
i.e., the major effort throughout the lifetime of
the project was devoted to collecting the detailed
properties of PL/1 and to their condensation in an
appropriate mathematical model.

The major aim of the project was the precise
definition of PL/1. Only recently we have started
to return to the original aim, namely the systematic
construction of implementations on the basis of a
given formal definition of the source language (see
the third section of this paper).

Three versions of the PL/1 definition have been
produced. The first (and incomplete) version was
finished by 1966, the third and last version by 1969.
In addition to PL/1, the definition method was
applied to ALGOL 60 [8], to BASIC [9] and to APL by
a group at the Carnegie-Mellon University.

In all above-mentioned instances the situation
is peculiar. Ideally, one would like to design a
programming language by designing an abstract
machine, thus using the formal framework as a design
tool. However, so far the languages to be described
existed already by virtue of a document and a
community interpreting this document. In this
situation the task is to find an underlying abstract
machine which corresponds to the understanding of
a group of people.

The following comments are intended to show the
motivation for certain technical decisions and some
of the technical problems of the PL/1 definition and
the specific solution within the Vienna Method.

One principle chosen for the PL/1 definition
was to give each constituent of the language a
direct interpretation. The translation of constituents of PL/1 into more primitive ones or a translation of the language into another more primitive
language was excluded as a means of definition.
There are two reasons for this decision. First, it
seemed that there are not many parts of PL/1 one
could eliminate in terms of more primitive constituents. Second, it was felt that a direct interpretation would mean more to the intuition of the
user of the definition, in other words, be more
economical for human minds than the indirect definition by means of a translation. The choice was
thus made with respect to the intended use of the
definition.

For other purposes, e.g., theoretical investi-
gation, it might well be that a translation is the
better way to go.

There is a part of the PL/1 definition called
the "translator." This term is misleading in view
of what has been said in the previous paragraph.
The "translator"-part of the definition specifies
a mapping from programs as represented by character
strings into abstract programs, which preserves the
essential linguistic structure. Thus there is no
elimination of certain types of phrases, such as
do-loops, etc.

Another subject that has caused considerable
discussion is the fact that the states of the
abstract PL/1 machine contain the program to be
interpreted, i.e., the program may be subject to
dynamic changes. We have seen no way to avoid the
inclusion of programs (or at least program pointers)
in the state because of two properties of PL/1:

1. the existence of goto statements, in
    particular goto statements to non-
    local labels,

2. the fact that certain actions must be
    specified to occur in unknown order

(arbitrary merging of actions).

The complication introduced into the definition by the goto-statement seems to correspond to the arguments against the use of goto-statements in well-structured programs. The goto statement destroys the correspondence between the linguistic structure of the program and the dynamic structure of the computation [4].

This is the pattern one would like to use in defining the meaning of a phrase-structured command: the state transition of the command is defined in terms of the state transitions corresponding to its immediate subphrases. The Vienna Definition in particular follows this pattern by specifying for each command either the corresponding state to state mapping (if the command was elementary), or the expansion in terms of the subphrases [11]. Goto statements have the following consequence: Parts of an expansion may become irrelevant if one of the subphrases happens to be a goto statement. One possibility to make an expansion irrelevant is to delete it. In order to be able to show the deletions, the parts potentially to be deleted must be parts of the state. Thus, we keep copies of program-parts in the state for the sole purpose of being able to delete them.

The influence of arbitrary merging of actions can be demonstrated by a simple example. It is assumed that F, G and H are parameterless function procedures with side effects. We consider the evaluation of the expression (F + (G + H)). Only the side effect of the expression evaluation is of concern but not the resulting value. Let f, g and h be the corresponding state transition functions. If the order of evaluation is left to right, the total state transition s( ) can clearly be expressed by:

$$s_1(\sigma) = h(g(\sigma))$$

$$s(\sigma) = s_1(f(\sigma))$$

It is even possible to express arbitrary ordering in the evaluation of operands by:

$$s_1(\sigma) \quad = \quad \begin{cases} \text{either} & h(g(\sigma)) \\ \text{or} & g(h(\sigma)) \end{cases}$$

$$s(\sigma) \quad = \quad \begin{cases} \text{either} & s_1(f(\sigma)) \\ \text{or} & f(s_1(\sigma)) \end{cases}$$

As a consequence, the evaluation of the expression would have at most four distinct possible successor states. But still the state transition of the entire phrase can be expressed in terms of the state transitions of the immediate subphrases. PL/1, however, requires the specification of arbitrarily merged evaluations of the individual primaries of expressions, i.e., there may be six distinct possible successor states of the given expression evaluation. The program is therefore kept in the state and the expansion mechanism is described explicitly as part of the computation ([11], chapter 6).

The state components other than the previously discussed control component are mainly concerned with the meaning of names, i.e., the information associated with declared identifiers of the program being executed. The structuring of this part of the state is a non-trivial problem. The attempt to define the structure of the state so that the meaning of identifiers can be correctly reflected gives the deepest insight into the programming language being defined. Going through this exercise we ourselves have been able to understand and clarify the meaning of PL/1. In particular, the study of sharing patterns reveals many important properties (two names share a certain piece of information if the two names refer to the same copy of that information). The question "what" is a variable in PL/1 and can be answered, according to the formal definition, completely and precisely and, most important, by comparatively simple rules (see [11], chapter 4.3.2). It may appear rather surprising that the

e.g., state transition function.

Together these elements form the basis of the formal definition method. So-called instructions and instruction definitions are notational abbreviations for functions and function definitions introduced to increase conciseness and readability. bility.

It is obvious that the abstract objects as introduced are suitable to exhibit the phrase structure of programs. It is less obvious that the same domain of objects can be conveniently identified with the states of the abstract machine as well. This choice was made for economic reasons, i.e., exactly the same definition tools can be used for programs and states. It turned out that the choice was a lucky one for most purposes; for a few problems, however, hierarchically structured objects are not the right solution. The major example for such an area is the part of the state by which the properties of PL/1 related to storage are modelled: the so-called storage component. Our problem arising with storage is that it is necessary to talk about partially overlapping parts of storage. Thus, the structuring that ought to be given to the storage component of the state is clearly not hierarchical. Furthermore, as far as the storage mapping and allocation are concerned most of the details are left open by PL/1 and only certain constraints have to be expressed. Therefore the properties of the storage part are given by axioms rather than by explicit definitions. The definition of the storage properties was one of the most difficult parts of the PL/1 definition. Therefore several different formulations may be found in the successive versions of the PL/1 definition. One specific formulation may be found in [11], chapter 5.

It is sometimes discussed whether the tree-structured objects introduced in our definition can be regarded as proper mathematical objects. I think we use our tree-structured objects for two purposes. We have used these objects where mathematicians would talk about n-tuples; and we use

objects where mathematicians would talk about
mappings. For example, instead of defining the
environment component of a state as a tree with
identifiers as selectors and unique names as components, we could equally well specify environments
to be mappings from identifiers into unique names.
For reasons of conciseness we would, however, have
to introduce a similar substitution operator, as
for objects, to transform mappings. Instead of
describing the total state of the abstract machine
as an object with certain immediate components one
could equally well define the state as an n-tuple
(n some not too large number). However, since the
structuring of the state is quite complicated, it is
convenient that the object provide a standard naming
convention (via selectors) for the elements of
tuples.

STUDY OF ISOLATED LANGUAGE FEATURES AND THEIR IMPLEMENTATIONS

This and the following section deal more with
subjects we would like to investigate than with
subjects that have been investigated in depth.

First of all, we would like to come back to the
original problem of the entire development, i.e.,
the systematic design of implementations. It is
obvious that the attempt to study the relation of,
e.g., the PL/1 definition with one of its implementations in toto is bound to fail, at least presently.
Thus we must look for appropriate, i.e., manageable,
subproblems. More precisely, instead of the study
of an entire language defined by an elaborate
abstract machine, we must study parts or features
of languages defined by the corresponding parts of
their defining abstract machine. There exist two
worked-out examples for such studies.

The one is the definition of the block concept
and its implementation by the display mechanism
[5]. The problem is to define the block concept
in isolation and prove the correctness of the above

mentioned implementation technique. To define the
block concept we assume an abstract machine, e.g.,
the PL/1 machine, but all state components which
are irrelevant for the resolution of the scope
problem are ignored. The state components which
are relevant for expressing the scope rules are just
a few (namely, the environment, the dump, and certain
parts of the denotation directory).

Then we distinguish four types of state transitions, namely those which correspond to block
entry, procedure call, block and procedure exit,
and finally all other state transitions which might
occur in the given abstract machine. The first
three are described explicitly by referring to the
state components relevant for the block concept; all
other state transitions are only constrained by a
few axioms, e.g., specifying that none of them will
change the environment component of the state. In
addition, it is necessary to specify parts of the
mechanisms used for the identifier references which
might occur during a computation.

In order to prove correctness of the implementation with respect to the above definition we have
formulated the implementation mechanism in a similar
way, i.e., as a part of an abstract machine. Thus
we specify the necessary state components (e.g.,
the pointers for the lexigraphic chain, etc.) and
define the state transitions with respect to these
state components as they ought to occur upon block
entry, procedure call, block exit, and we then
specify the necessary constraints for all other
state components. Finally, the mechanism used for
referencing identifiers is specified.

What has to be shown in order to prove correctness is the equivalence of the reference mechanisms
in both, the defining machine and in the implementation.

The proof of a subproblem [10] and the complete
and more elegant proof in [7] succeed by combining
the defining machine and the implementation into
one abstract machine (i.e., by combining the states

and the state transition into a twin machine) and
by a subsequent induction over the states as produced by the state transitions, showing that the
two reference mechanisms yield the same result
independent of the state.

The second example for a study of an isolated
aspect of programming language has been carried out
by H. Bekic and K. Walk and is concerned with the
storage structure, -mapping and -allocation of ALGOL
60, ALGOL 68 and PL/1 and the comparison of these
three languages in this specific area [3].

How much one can generalize these examples is
an open question. Certainly, we don't see how all
the aspects of an entire language like PL/1 can be
analyzed in analogy to the above indicated examples.

One of my personal aims is to arrive at a more
systematic and respectable way to teach languages
and implementations. For this purpose the above
mentioned examples have already served well.

ON SOFTWARE DEVICES

In the previous chapter it was indicated how
parts of abstract machines may serve to describe
parts of programming languages. In this section we
will accept another criterion to take abstract
machines apart, namely the formal structure of the
individual state components and their respective
elementary state transitions.

Examples for different types of components
within the PL/1 machine are:

1. Directories: mappings, usually with
corresponding elementary state transitions, which
allow the required update, and the necessary access
function;

2. Stacks: with the usual transition function
and access function;

3. Storage part: with the transitions to reflect allocation and assignment, and the access function corresponding to storage references.

Such parts, i.e., states, elementary state transitions and access functions are called *devices*.

On the basis of a description of the essential properties of such a device one may study the possible implementations on given machines. In doing so, one would prepare the nuts and bolts for implementations of abstract machines involving such devices.

One could also study the possible compositions of devices and the respective compositions of their implementations and thus provide for general construction principles, i.e., the rules for use of devices.

In formulating the essential properties of a device one should not rely on a particular programming language. Any process expressed by a particular programming language is bound to remain within the limits of the underlying machine, i.e., is bound to be expressed in terms of the set of states and available state transitions of the underlying machine. Thus, the use of a particular programming language may force one to exhibit more detail than is essential in a device and may also force unnatural representations of states.

Instead it is proposed to discuss devices in terms of ordinary mathematical tools. This freedom from any particular programming language would seem to allow the choice of the adequate level of abstraction.

The following example specifying a stack device and one of its implementations is intended to illustrate the above general discussion.

The Stack Device

A basic set G of elements to be stacked is assumed. Interpreting the term "stack" in its usual technical sense, the following properties must be taken as essential:

(a) The top element of the stack must be accessible.

(b) It must be possible to add a new element out of G on top of the stack.

(c) It must be possible to remove the top element from the stack.

The following constitutes the mathematical formulation of the stack device.

g, g_1, g_2 denote arbitrary elements of G

States of the Machine

s, s'   denote arbitrary states of the machine (stacks); the internal structure of these states need not be further analyzed

Ø   denotes a specific stack, the empty stack

The empty stack will usually be used as the *initial state*.

Elementary Functions

top(s)   yields the top element; (top (Ø) is undefined)

push(s,g) = s' yields a new stack s' with g as the top element

pop(s) = s'   yields a new stack s' with the
                 top element removed.

The following axioms state the relation between
the above functions formally.

Axioms

(5)   top(push(s,g)) = g

(6)   pop(push(s,g)) = s

The functions "push" and "pop" are state transition functions, the function "top" is an access
function specifying that any implementation must
give access to the top element of the stack whereas
the other element may be inaccessible. The function
"push" assumes that there is an element g to be
stacked, which will usually not be part of the stack
considered. The function "top" and the second
argument of "push" constitute the linkage points of
the device if it is combined with other devices.

A usual implementation of the stack device for
fixed length elements is shown below. The machine
on which the device is to be implemented is assumed
to have a linear array M of storage cells as its
working storage and an index register IR with the
usual facilities for address modification. The
constant address i_0 is assumed as the base address
of the stack.

The table of correspondence given in Figure 3
shows the implementation.

It is easy to verify that the implementation
has the desired properties in terms of the axioms.

ABSTRACTION	IMPLEMENTATION
s	$IR, M[i_0+1],\ldots,M[i_0+IR]$ where $IR \geq 0$
Ø	$IR = 0$
top(s)	$M[i_0 + IR]$
push(s,g)	$IR := IR + 1;$ $M[i_0 + IR] := g;$
pop(s)	$IR := IR - 1$

Figure 3

Implementation of the Stack Device

REFERENCES

[1] Bekic, H., "Mechanical Transformation Rules
     for the Reduction of ALGOL to Primitive Lan-
     guage and their Use in Defining the Compiler
     Function," *Lab. Report LR 25.3.007*, IBM
     Laboratory Vienna, 1964.

[2] ———, "On the Formal Definition of Programming
     Languages," *Proceedings of the International
     Computing Symposium Bonn*, 1970.

[3] ———, and Walk, K., "Formalization of Storage
     Properties," *Lab. Report LR 25.5.034*, IBM
     Laboratory Vienna, 1970, also in Springer
     Lecture Note Series.

[4] Dijkstra, E.W., "Notes on Structured Program-
     ming," *T.H. Report 70-Wsk-03*, Technical Uni-
     versity Eindhoven, EWD 249, 1970.

[5]   ——, "Recursive Programming," *Numer.*
       Mathematik 2, 1960, No. 5.

[6]   Elgot, C.C., Robinson, A., "Random-Access,
       Stored Program Machines: An Approach to
       Programming Languages," *JACM 11,* 1964, No. 4,
       365-399.

[7]   Jones, C.B., Lucas, P., "Proving Correctness
       of Implementation Techniques," *Technical
       Report TR 25.110,* 1970, IBM Laboratory Vienna,
       also in Springer Lecture Note Series, No. 188,
       Springer Verlag, Berlin-Hamburg-New York, 1971.

[8]   Lauer, P.E., "Formal Definition of ALGOL 60,"
       Technical Report TR 25.121, IBM Laboratory
       Vienna, 1971.

[9]   Lee, J., "Formal Definition of BASIC,"
       Publication No. TN/CS/00013, University of
       Massachusetts, 1969.

[10]   Lucas, P., "Two Constructive Realizations of
       the Block Concept and Their Equivalence,"
       ULD-Version 2, TR 25.085, IBM Laboratory Vienna,
       1968.

[11]   Lucas, P., Walk, K., "On the Formal Definition
       of PL/1," *Ann. Rev. in Aut. Progr. 6,* Part 3,
       1969, Pergamon Press, 105-181.

[12]   McCarthy, J., "Towards a Mathematical Science
       of Computation," *Information Processing 1962*
       (J. Popplewell, Ed), 1963, Amsterdam.

[13]   ——, "A Formal Description of a Subset of
       ALGOL," *Formal Language Description Languages
       for Computer Programming* (T.B. Steel, Ed),
       North-Holland Publ. Comp., 1966, Amsterdam.

[14]   Walk, K., "Modelling of Storage Properties of
       Higher-Level Languages," *ACM Symposium,*
       University of Florida, 1971.

REMARKS ON ONE-ARGUMENT PROGRAM SCHEMES

Calvin C. Elgot
IBM Thomas J. Watson Research Center

A point of view concerning one-argument program schemes is outlined in an informal way.

There are notions of one-argument program schemes (for example those considered by Ianov and Rutledge, cf. [II], [JR]) which have the effect of fixing attention on the sequencing aspect of programs to the exclusion of all other aspects. For example, any structure external memory may have is ignored.

These schemes may be roughly described as constructed out of atomic parts at least of the following types:

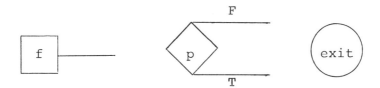

These atomic parts are interconnected in a way
which we assume is familiar. In addition, one part
is designated as "begin."

    A simple but significant example of a program
scheme is this:

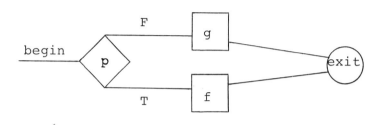

If p is interpreted as a predicate, i.e., as a
function $p:X \to \{T,F\}$ and f,g are interpreted as
functions $f,g:X \to X$, where X is any set, then the
scheme is interpreted as calculating the function
$h:X \to X$ which satisfies:

$$(1) \quad (x)h = \begin{cases} (x)f & \text{if} & (x)p = T \\ (x)g & \text{if} & (x)p = F, \text{ where } x\varepsilon X. \end{cases}$$

    Let $p':X \to X \times \{T,F\}$ be the function satisfy-
ing: $(x)p' = (x,(x)p)$ and let $(f,g):X \times \{T,F\} \to X$
be the function satisfying $(x,T)(f,g) = (x)f$ and
$(x,F)(f,g) = (x)g$. Then the function h defined
above may be described as the composite

$$h: X \xrightarrow{\quad p' \quad} X \times \{T,F\} \xrightarrow{\quad (f,g) \quad} X, \text{ i.e.}$$

$$(2) \qquad\qquad h = p'(f,g) \qquad .$$

    Thus, in a programming language predicates

p:X → {T,F} may be replaced by *decisions*
p':X → X X {T,F} and conditional expressions such
as (1) may be replaced by composition as in (2).

　　　If we take this course, we may as well permit
program schemes such as

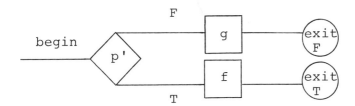

　　　To describe the function computed (under any
interpretation), we define

　　　f ⊕ g:X X {T,F} → X X {T,F}

　　　(x,T)(f ⊕ g) = (x)f

　　　(x,F)(f ⊕ g) = (x)g.

Then the function computed by the interpreted program scheme is the composite

$$(3)\quad k:X \xrightarrow{\;\;p'\;\;} X\ X\ \{T,F\} \xrightarrow{\;\;f\oplus g\;\;} X\ X\ \{T,F\},$$

　　　　i.e.　　　　k = p'(f ⊕ g)　　.

　　　Formula (3) suggests expanding "program scheme"
to permit two "begins" and defining a notion of composition of schemes so that the scheme above is the
composite of the following two schemes

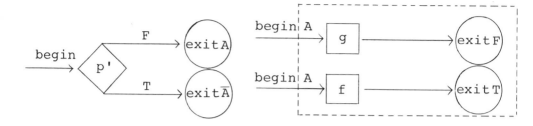

where A is T or F and $\overline{A}$ is the other.

If we define $\mu : X \ X \ \{T,F\} \to X$

$$(x,T)\mu = x \quad , \quad (x,F)\mu = x \qquad \text{then}$$

$$h = k \ \mu \quad .$$

These considerations suggest merging the predicate and operation parts of a scheme and lifting the restriction to at most two edges to obtain atomic parts of the type

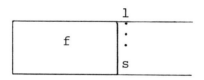

Figure 1

Such an atomic part may be interpreted as a function $f : X \to X \ X \ \{1,\ldots,s\}$. These considerations also suggest permitting the designations "begin 1,..., begin n" to atomic parts and permitting exits 1 to p for various n, p.

One further remark of a different kind. As is

quite well known, interpreted program schemes (with
cycles)may compute partial functions even though
the atomic parts are interpreted as (total) functions. By introducing partial functions at an
early stage, it is possible to describe the partial
function computed by an interpreted program scheme
without resort to an intervening notion of "computation." Namely, we replace the function
$f:X \rightarrow X \ X \ \{1,\ldots,s\}$ by s partial functions
$f_i:X \rightarrow X$, $i = 1,\ldots,s$ defined by

$$(4) \quad f_i:X \xrightarrow{\quad f \quad} X \ X \ \{1,\ldots,s\} \xrightarrow{\quad X \ X \ i^{-1} \quad} X$$

where $X \ X \ i^{-1}$ takes (x,i) into x and is otherwise
undefined. These s partial functions have domains
which are pairwise disjoint.

The atomic part Figure 1 may then be replaced
by the atomic part below

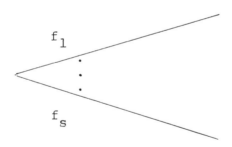

Figure 2

yielding what is called an "exit automaton" in
[CE1]. Suppose the exit automaton has one beginning node and one exit and is constructed out of
non-exit atomic parts solely of the Figure 2 type.
By the behavior of the exit automaton let us mean,
as usual, the set of all words on the set of
"letters" $\{f_1,\ldots,f_s\}$ which are labels of paths f
from the beginning node to the exit.

Let P be a (one begin, one exit) program
scheme built solely out of Figure 1. Let P' be the
exit automaton which results by replacing Figure 1
by Figure 2 and let $|P'|$ be the behavior of the
exit automaton. If we interpret f as a function
$f:X \to X \times \{1,\ldots,s\}$, P is interpreted as computing
a partial function $P:X \to X$. If we now interpret
the letters f_i as partial functions $f_i:X \to X$
according to (4), the words represent partial
functions by interpreting juxtaposition as compo-
sition and $|P'|$ represents the partial function
$|P'|:X \to X$ by taking the union of the partial
functions represented by words in $|P'|$. Then
(theorem) the partial function $P:X \to X$ and
$|P'|:X \to X$ are the same.

These remarks may serve as intuitive background for the more mathematical discussions in
[CE1] and [CE2].

REFERENCES

[II]   Ianov, I.I., "The Logical Schemes of Algor-
       ithms," English translation in: *Problems of
       Cybernetics 1*, Pergamon Press, 1960, 82-140.

[JR]   Rutledge, J.D., "On Ianov's Program Schemata,"
       JACM 11, 1964, 1-9.

[CE1] Elgot, C.C., "The Common Algebraic Structure
       of Exit-Automata and Machines," *Computing*,
       Vol. 6, Fasc 3-4, 1970, 349-370.

[CE2] ——, C.C., "Algebraic Theories and Program
       Schemes," *Symposium on Semantics of Algor-
       ithmic Languages*, edited by E. Engeler,
       Springer-Verlag.

LATTICE THEORY, DATA TYPES AND SEMANTICS

Dana Scott
Princeton University

An abstract theory of finite approximation and infinite limits is described in general terms with the aid of lattice theory. The concepts apply to the effective construction of a variety of spaces (data-types), including function spaces, which enables them to be used as mathematical value spaces for semantic interpretations of high-level computer languages.

In effect, I shall speak today against discrete mathematics. I find that the word *discrete* is often used as a catch word in blurbs about computer science programs, in catalogues and announcements to give a more "practical" sound to course descriptions. Of course, that does not mean that I am against studying finite objects. I realize perfectly well that people can spend their lives doing interesting and important things about combinatorics, finite groups, finite projective planes, and other finite structures. But it seems to me that there is something *beyond* those finite structures, something we cannot do without in our mathematical thinking.

I ask you, for example, to consider a circle
Is the circle simply a polygon with a very large
number of sides? Or is the circle something more
than that? Certainly Archimedes used polygons with
large numbers of sides to calculate to an excellent
degree of *approximation* certain numbers having to
do with circles. But still, the circle goes *beyond*,
or is somehow a *limit of*, those approximations.

Now you will quickly remind me that there is
something beyond discrete mathematics: the arbitrary
mathematical structures, the arbitrary infinite sets.
And I answer that I also wish to speak against the
arbitrary. I realize perfectly well that people
can spend their lives studying infinite or inaccessible cardinal numbers, very large ordinal numbers,
topological spaces of peculiar sorts. I do not
deny that those structures are there. But I am
going to try to argue for some concepts intermediate
between the discrete and the arbitrary, concepts
which I shall call *continuous*. I shall attempt to
sell the philosophy that the intermediate, continuous
stage is an appropriate vantage point for studying
a variety of notions that have come from recursive
function theory, from logic, from numerical analysis,
and from the study of computer languages.

The λ-calculus is a good example: it arose
from a study of logic. Professor Church, for example,
had hoped at one time that this approach to logic
through a general calculus of functions was going to
solve the problems of naive set theory[2] He thought
that he had invented a new system of logic which
was to accomplish what Frege's unfortunately inconsistent theory was meant to. Alas at a certain
moment, I think when both Kleene and Rosser had
practically finished writing their theses using
Church's system of logic, they discovered that the
new system was also inconsistent. What Kleene had
to do was throw out all of the parts of his work
that depended upon notions of the general type-free
theory. What he had left, of course, was the
beginning of his approach to recursive functions.
He took over many of the ideas from the λ-calculus
and used them year after year in important papers

on recursive function theory.

As was mentioned this morning, there is a way
in which you can think of the λ-calculus as arising
from programming languages: namely, it's a very
isolated, very purified part of the theory of
procedures. A λ-expression may be thought of as a
procedure in which we pass only one parameter at a
time. Moreover, it generally takes a procedure as
an argument and produces a procedure as a value.
It may not sound as though we are getting anywhere
at all with that concept, but if you have worked
with the λ-calculus and know about the combinations
that you can introduce by spreading out the occurrences of the variables in ingenious orders, then
you know you can make these λ-expressions combine
in quite interesting ways. Professor Curry has
spent many years in discussing those kinds of
combinations, motivated originally by the desire to
study the mechanism of *substitution*. Rosser discovered, for example, that in such a pure calculus
you can reinterpret the arithmetic of the integers
by using certain kinds of iterators to stand for
the numbers. In this way all of elementary recursive function theory, for example, can be developed
in this very pure calculus[3]

The study of λ-calculus, however, has been very
much pushed on discrete level. That is to say,
instead of trying to interpret what the λ-expressions
mean in themselves, people have merely given *rules
of calculation* for reducing one λ-expression to
another. As a matter of fact, the kinds of rules
proposed are very reminiscent of what one has to go
through in interpreting the behaviors of programs
in various programming languages. Indeed, Peter
Landin and others made just this connection with
the kind of reductions you have to do in the λ-
calculus a basis of a study of programming languages[4]

Now I do not wish to argue against the interest
of rules of reduction. There are many ways in which
you can arrange those rules, and in the talks this
morning several different ways of reducing the
expressions were discussed. Some methods of

reduction perform much more reduction than others.
For purposes of some programming languages even the
rules of Church and Curry were considered too general, for if you allow reductions at every point of
the expression, it might waste a lot of time in
reducing unnecessary parts. So there are several
modified procedures to assure a practical and
efficient reduction to values.[5] In some sense I am
willing to say that all of these reduction procedures — handling the expressions by substituting
one expression into the other in appropriate ways —
all those methods are correct. But I feel there is
something more to λ-expressions than what is embodied
in those rules. I deny for the sake of argument
that the meaning of the λ-calculus is given by
reduction rules.

As it turns out, if λ-expressions have *normal
forms* (if they can be reduced as far as possible
without getting into an infinite loop of never-
ending reductions), then the normal-form expressions
are in a way discrete. At least they are discrete
with respect to each other. That is to say, if you
take two distinct normal forms, then they do in fact
represent discretely distinguishable objects. The
proof is by an interesting theorem of Corrado Boehm[6]
which shows that, given two λ-expressions F and G
with distinct normal forms, there is an algorithm
to effectively write down a list of arguments
X_0, X_1,...,X_n to which these λ-expressions can be
applied to obtain distinguishable results. Specifically, if A and B are also given in advance, then
the arguments will be such that $F(X_0)...(X_n)$ reduces
to A while $G(X_0)...(X_n)$ reduces to B. Therefore,
if you were ever tempted to say that F and G were
supposed to be the same, you would involve yourself
in a contradiction: obviously from the equality of
F and G you would be able to prove the equality of
any two λ-expressions. Thus Boehm has shown that
λ-expressions in normal form really are different,
and the formal, manipulative rules of the λ-calculus
are complete for expressions in normal form. However, for expressions that do not have normal forms,
the situation is not so clear.

Curry likes to use expressions that have no normal form, while Church did not at one time. Since Church's system fell into inconsistency, he thought that the reason lay with these terrible expressions without normal form. They were undoubtedly supposed to be "meaningless," so he oriented some of his calculi toward excluding these expressions, considering expressions meaningful only if they had normal form. Well, under my present point of view, I would like to assert that this attitude is wrong. I will say that *every* expression of the λ- calculus has a perfectly good meaning. The meaning will not always be discovered by the reduction rules, however. We shall have to introduce a new method in order to find it. There will be expressions not reducible to one another according to the well-known rules of the λ-calculus which, under my interpretation, do in fact have the same meaning. For example, there are two versions of what Curry calls the *paradoxical combinator* which are not reducible to one another, but which David Park was able to show under my interpretation have the same meaning.[7]

It should not be surprising that there will be sameness of meaning which escapes a certain discretely stated system of reduction rules. The objective of the λ-calculus was to represent "logical" functions of a very general sort. So an equation between such expressions is a *functional equation*. A functional equation always tells you an infinite number of facts: it tells you that for any argument the left hand function applied to that argument gives the same value as the right-hand function applied to that argument. As we know, in formal systems incompleteness a la Gödel arises, and it is in general not going to be possible to effectively enumerate all true equations of a functional sort. Thus the fact that the usual rules for the λ-calculus are incomplete should not come as any shock.

*   *   *

This completes my introductory remarks. Before I discuss the construction of models for the λ-calculus, I would be glad to answer questions.

Peter Wegner: *In my talk I was trying to say that you might associate different, equally valid, notions of meaning with objects of the lambda calculus. For instance, operational meaning defined by reduction rules is a different kind of meaning from your meaning, and emphasizes different attributes of the associated objects. Would you be prepared to grant the validity of different types of meaning, or would you say that your sense of meaning is more basic than any other?*

Answer: I claim that my sense of meaning is more basic. The manipulative theory of reduction is an often very effective way of understanding the meaning of expressions, similarly with the usual formal systems. Once you can write down a formal proof in black and white, you have some hope of following the steps and really seeing why the theorem happens to be true. It is the same with λ-calculus.

Wegner: *Don't you think that renaming and reduction tell you something about the λ-calculus that your sense of meaning does not? It tells you something concrete.*

Answer: Take the idea of reduction, for example. It means simply that if you define a function according to a certain formula, then in order to evaluate the function you have to substitute in the expression that denotes argument for the variable. That is all that reduction is, and that is the basic way in which we define functions. According to my theory of meaning I shall validate, as one of the first steps that has to be carried out, the fact that this reduction rule is correct. Namely, if you take the meaning as a function of a λ-expression λx.[...x...], and apply that function to an argument a, you will discover that the meaning of λx.[...x...] applied to a is the same as the meaning of the substitution [...a...]. Thus, the reduction rule you mentioned is just one of the first things which you have to validate in order to make sure that your system of functional definition behaves the way you intended it to behave.

Wegner: *What about the two forms of the definition of factorial?*

Answer: There may be many different power series for the sine function. When you look at books on numerical analysis they suggest ways of finding better and better power series to make things converge faster. But no one denies that all the different power series still add up to the same function.

Wegner: *I don't know what the connection is between this particular transcendental function and the pure λ-calculus. You brought this in as another example, but I don't see the connection to the λ-calculus. Could you start from the renaming and reduction rules and validate your type of meaning from that?*

Answer: No, as I tried to explain there are two different versions of Curry's Y operator, both of which are some kind of λ-expression which when applied to a function allows you to reduce that expression to the given function applied to the same expression. If any λ-expression Y has that property, it may be called a *fixed-point operator*. The two distinct λ-expressions I have in mind are called Y_0 and Y_1. These are not equal by renaming and reduction. However, when you take the meaning which I assign to the expression in my model, then (as I mentioned before) David Park proved that they are equal in meaning.[8] The λ-expressions in question are as follows: Let

$$X = \lambda x.f(x(x)),$$
$$Y_0 = \lambda f.X(X), \text{ and}$$
$$Y_1 = Y_0(\lambda y.\lambda f.f(y(f))).$$

Then by reduction:

$$Y_0 = \lambda f.f(Y_0(f)), \text{ and}$$
$$Y_1 = \lambda f.f(Y_1(f)),$$

which looks the same, but it is not and can never be made the same by renaming and reduction.[9]

We may be able to understand the situation better with reference to the incompleteness theorem. Gödel showed that for a certain formal system there is a true statement which is not provable as a theorem. You can now fix that up by adding that true sentence as a new axiom, because Gödel's argument shows you why it is true. But then his argument also reapplies: he can find yet another statement which is not provable with the help of the new axiom. So you are always stuck no matter how you axiomatize theories effectively; no matter how you give "reduction" rules for a step-by-step discrete handling of expressions transforming one into another. If your calculus involves concepts of power not beyond the strictly finite (Boolean algebra say, is just the calculus of zeros and ones), then you can get all equivalences by discrete rules in view of the discreteness of the values. There are some other intermediate cases where rules will allow you to obtain all true equivalences. If you go to a powerful enough calculus, however, a calculus that has something essential to do with functional equations, then the type of incompleteness like Gödel's theorem takes over: There will be no effective axiomatization.

Calvin Elgot: *Is there a qualitative difference between the meaning of those formulas which have normal form and those that do not?*

Answer: I do not know if I can put my finger on some qualitative difference. The best we have at the moment is the theorem of Boehm which shows that distinct normal forms could not possibly be equal. But I have not been able to discover as yet some "mathematical" quality of the values of the expressions without normal form.

*   *   *

The way by which I arrived at my theory of meaning for the λ-calculus was to go back to the idea of *finite approximation*. The method also applies to many more complex languages. Just as we approximate the circle by polygons, I say that there is a general theory of finite approximation and that there are many types of objects that can be achieved as *limits* of approximations. Just as we smooth out the polygons to obtain a circle in the limit, so in other structures we can pass to the limit to find objects that are much smoother than any of their finite approximations can ever be. One aspect of the "smoothness" that these limit objects exhibit might turn out to be the beautiful equations which they satisfy, just as the transcendental functions satisfy beautiful equations which polynomials cannot.

In order to set up this theory of approximation we can begin by thinking about an *approximation relation* in a qualitative sense. If this theory turns out to be any good, and if we are sufficiently pleased with the beauty of the smooth objects that are so obtained, it may very well be that we can go on to discuss degrees of approximation and, for limits, rates of convergence. At the moment, however, I do not know how to accomplish this feat in a general theory. I only know how to give a definition of convergence based upon the behavior of objects under a qualitative sense of approximation.

The mathematical theory is based on the very simple idea that the approximation relation $\sqsubseteq$ should be a *partial ordering*, not just any such structure, but one in which you can take limits (Figure 1). Partial orderings are conveniently sketched in diagrams in the familiar way (Figure 2). The relationship $x \sqsubseteq y$ can intuitively be read as: x *approximates* y. We think of x as *worse* and y as *better*, but we do not say how *close* x is to y. You

Dana Scott

$$X \sqsubseteq Y$$

X APPROXIMATES Y

THIS IS A QUALITATIVE RELATION THAT
IS MEANT TO IMPLY THAT X IS CONSISTENT
WITH Y. THE APPROXIMATION MAY BE EITHER
GOOD OR BAD.

PROPERTIES:

(1) $x \sqsubseteq x$
(2) $x \sqsubseteq y \sqsubseteq z$ IMPLIES $x \sqsubseteq z$
(3) $x \sqsubseteq y \sqsubseteq x$ IMPLIES $x = y$

Figure 1

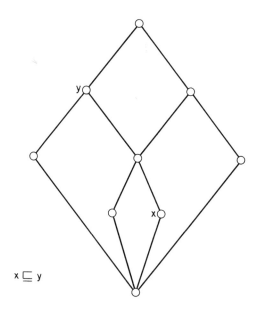

$x \sqsubseteq y$

Figure 2

A Diagram of a Finite Lattice

may think of these objects as "containing" information — not complete information, only partial
information. Thus x $\sqsubseteq$ y means roughly that the
information contained in y includes that of x: that
is why y is better.

One of the main objects I had in mind in
developing this theory was to have a convenient
theory of functions. These will be very much like
partial functions, because the value of f(x) may be
an object containing only "incomplete" information.
What is especially convenient is that by this plan
we do not have to ever say that f(x) is "undefined,"
rather we can say f(x) has a value which is incomplete in some sense. In fact, if we want, we can
introduce into the partial ordering the totally
incomplete object $\bot$, where $\bot \sqsubseteq$ x always holds.
Thus f(x) = $\bot$ means that f(x) is undefined in the
usual sense. It has turned out very handy also to
allow many shades of "definedness," hence the
partial ordering.

Consideration of the conveniences of functions,
especially considerations of a topological sort which
enter when limits are required, led me further to
assume that the partial ordering is a *lattice*.
Before I started this study I really did not intend
to get into lattices. But, when I did I found my-
self forced into them. I found that there are many
more interesting lattices than I ever imagined. Of
course I knew before about such lattices as Boolean
algebras. I knew about the lattice of subspaces of
a linear space and the connection between lattices
and projective geometries. I knew about modular
lattices that failed to be distributive. Some of
those examples were either set-theoretical lattices
where the lattice structure did not actually tell you
too much, or they were particularly oriented toward
algebra and had rather special properties in view of
their algebraic genesis. But recently I found that
there are a multitude of other lattices closely
associated with topological spaces. Furthermore,
interesting and useful properties of convergence
and continuity can find expression in terms of a
lattice-theoretic terminology in a very simple way.[10]

One requirement for a good theory of functions is the possibility of extending the domain of definition of a function. A closer study of how to obtain extensions will bring out the necessity for the lattice structure. I cannot go too deeply into details today, but you can imagine that the question of bounds to subsets of the partial ordering will come up.[11] In fact, we are going to have to assume that the whole set of elements is bounded above by an element $\top$ where $x \sqsubseteq \top$ always holds. We can call $\bot$ "bottom" and $\top$ "top" (Figure 3). Thinking of $\bot$ as the "undefined" element, we will have to take $\top$ as being "overdefined" or somehow "inconsistent" in the sense of containing too much information. The

$\top$ = THE TOP ELEMENT

$\bot$ = THE BOTTOM ELEMENT

$\top$ IS OVERDETERMINED WHILE $\bot$ IS UNDERTERMINED.

PROPERTIES:

(1) $x \sqsubseteq \top$
(2) $\bot \sqsubseteq x$

Figure 3

"good" elements will be somewhat less than $\top$. Besides this we will want to assume that any two elements x and y have *least upper bounds* (joins) and *greatest lower bounds* (meets) denoted by $x \sqcup y$ and $x \sqcap y$, respectively. We can think of $x \sqcup y$ being obtained by joining together the "bits" of information contained in x and y (Figure 4); while with $x \sqcap y$ we take what is common to the two (Figure 5), but this is a rather rough description. I am sure you are familiar with how these operations look in a lattice diagram.

To get at the important idea of a limit in the lattice formulation one does nothing more than to

$$X \sqcup Y$$

THE JOIN OF X AND Y

THIS OPERATION COMBINES THE INFOR-
MATION OF X AND Y GIVING A LEAST UPPER
BOUND TO THE ELEMENTS.

PROPERTIES:

(1) $X \sqsubseteq X \sqcup Y$
(2) $Y \sqsubseteq X \sqcup Y$
(3) $X, Y \sqsubseteq Z$ IMPLIES $X \sqcup Y \sqsubseteq Z$

THE EQUATION $X \sqcup Y = \top$ MEANS THAT
THE ELEMENTS ARE INCONSISTENT.

Figure 4

$$X \sqcap Y$$

THE MEET OF X AND Y

THIS OPERATION WEAKENS THE INFOR-
MATION OF X AND Y GIVING A GREATEST
LOWER BOUND TO THE ELEMENTS.

PROPERTIES:

(1) $X \sqcap Y \sqsubseteq X$
(2) $X \sqcap Y \sqsubseteq Y$
(3) $Z \sqsubseteq X, Y$ IMPLIES $Z \sqsubseteq X \sqcap Y$

THE EQUATION $X \sqcap Y = \bot$ MEANS THAT
THE ELEMENTS ARE INDEPENDENT.

Figure 5

take the least upper bound of a set of elements.
That is, if we have some sort of lattice and a set
of elements, they might be spread out in the
"horizontal" direction, or they might be somewhat
ordered "vertically" among themselves. In certain
cases the least upper bound can be considered as the
limit of this set of elements. You have to be just
a little bit careful in thinking about the limiting
process here. It is best to say that the least
upper bound of a set of elements is properly called
the limit only when the set is *directed*. This means
that every finite subset of the set has an upper
bound in the set. Note that for any set the least
upper bound of the set is properly described as a
limit of the finite join: The finite joins are
"finite" approximations to the ultimate join of
the whole set. A typical example of a directed set
is an infinite set of elements which form a chain:
each term approximates the next, say $x_n \sqsubseteq x_{n+1}$.
In this special case we can write the limit as

$$\bigsqcup_{n=0}^{\infty} x_n$$

For general sets X the least upper bound is written
as $\bigsqcup X$; thus all our lattices are to be complete
lattices (Figure 6). In applications you generally
have only to consider these simplest countable
limits; just as in the ordinary calculus you have
only to use infinite sequences to get the things
you want. But you can easily put it more abstractly,
if you enjoy doing that sort of thing.

Now, I have not yet explained to you how to
define these lattices. What I assert is that there
are a good number of these lattices and useful
functions on them — if you look at the right kind
of functions. We need some examples. If you like,
you can stick to the *discrete domain* where there are
no limits available. In the picture we see a lattice
N involving one top and one bottom element and an
infinite number of discretely separated elements
which we can identify with the integers (Figure 7).
It is not possible to take any interesting limits

$$\sqcup X$$

THE JOIN OF THE SET X

THIS OPERATION COMBINES THE INFOR-
MATION OF ALL THE ELEMENTS OF THE SET X
GIVING A LEAST UPPER BOUND TO THE ELEMENTS.

PROPERTIES:

(1) $x \sqsubseteq \sqcup X$, FOR ALL $x \varepsilon X$
(2) $x \sqsubseteq z$, FOR ALL $x \varepsilon X$, IMPLIES $\sqcup X \sqsubseteq z$

Figure 6

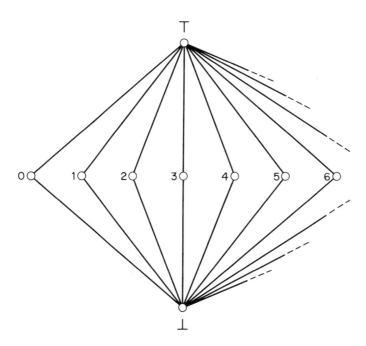

Figure 7

The Lattice N

in this lattice; because if you start at the bottom and try to push upwards to move information, you move up all of a sudden with one jump to a perfectly defined integer, say 3. Then if you try to push any further, you go at once too far and get to the top. We have the underdetermined integer, the perfect integers, and the overdetermined integer. There is nothing else in between. There is no way to get limits here. But this is just one example of a lattice of the kind I have in mind.

A lattice that is much more interesting from the point of view of sequences of approximations is the lattice [N → N] of integer-valued functions on the integers (Figure 8). But just which functions

AS A SET [N → N] IS THE SET OF ALL MONOTONIC FUNCTIONS F:N → N. WE DEFINE ⊑ ON THIS SET BY:

F ⊑ G IFF F(X) ⊑ G(X), FOR ALL X∈N.

THE REST OF THE LATTICE IS UNIQUELY DETERMINED, AND INDEED:

$$T(x) = T \qquad\qquad \bot(x) = \bot$$

$$(F \sqcup G)(x) = F(x) \sqcup G(x)$$
$$(F \sqcap G)(x) = F(x) \sqcap G(x)$$

FOR ALL X∈N, ALL F,G ∈ [N → N].

Figure 8

do we take? Since N is itself a lattice, the functions cannot be quite arbitrary. Assume all functions to be considered *preserve* the approximation relation. This means that whenever x ⊑ y, then f(x) ⊑ f(y), for f to be an allowed function. Abstractly f is required to be *monotonic*. Intuitively we reason that the more you increase the information content of the argument, the more you increase the information contained in the value — at least this is a

reasonable assumption if a function is going to be
anything like a computable function. And to be
able to have a general theory of computable functions
is part of the over-all program. For [N → N] we take
all monotonic functions; in the case of more general
lattices a further restriction is required which will
be explained in a moment.

Functions f,g ε [N → N] can easily be compared
as to "goodness" or "determinateness." We write
f ⊑ g to mean that f(x) ⊑ g(x) holds for all arguments x. That is, f approximates g if and only if
the approximation relation holds argumentwise.
(This definition is adopted in general lattices too.)
Of course the constant function g(x) ≡ ⊤ is "too
good" and the constant function f(x) ≡ ⊥ is the
"worst." Indeed the functions in [N → N] form a
lattice, as can easily be proved.

In Figure 9 I have sketched a table of a
sequence of monotonic functions f_0, f_1, f_2, ..., f_n,
..., where we have $f_n \sqsubseteq f_{n+1}$. This sequence of
distinct functions is approaching a limit, as you
can see. Each column in the table represents an
imperfect function, but the limit function

$$g = \bigsqcup_{n=0}^{\infty} f_n$$

is quite perfect, and possibly of interest to some
of us.

Another example of a lattice can be derived
from the real numbers. First you have the ordinary
real numbers sitting there in perfection along the
real line. But then you can think about how to
approximate these numbers. One way to do it is by
giving upper and lower limits to a number that you
might be thinking of. Usually when you specify
those approximations you use rational upper and
lower limits but that is not strictly necessary.
In other words, in the picture we see the real line
supplemented by a lattice structure formed out of

	F_0	F_1	F_2	F_3	F_4	F_5	F_6	F_7	F_8	_ _	G
T	⊥	0	T	T	T	T	T	T	T	....	T
0	⊥	0	0	0	0	0	0	0	0	....	0
1	⊥	⊥	1	1	1	1	1	1	1	....	1
2	⊥	⊥	⊥	4	4	4	4	4	4	....	4
3	⊥	⊥	⊥	⊥	9	9	9	9	9	....	9
4	⊥	⊥	⊥	⊥	⊥	16	16	16	16	....	16
5	⊥	⊥	⊥	⊥	⊥	⊥	25	25	25	....	25
6	⊥	⊥	⊥	⊥	⊥	⊥	⊥	36	36	....	36
7	⊥	⊥	⊥	⊥	⊥	⊥	⊥	⊥	49	....	49
8	⊥	⊥	⊥	⊥	⊥	⊥	⊥	⊥	⊥	....	64
N	⊥	⊥	⊥	⊥	⊥	⊥	⊥	⊥	⊥		N^2
⊥	⊥	⊥	⊥	⊥	⊥	⊥	⊥	⊥	⊥		⊥

$$\bigsqcup_{M = 0}^{\infty} F_M = G$$

Figure 9

A Limit in $[N \rightarrow N]$

intervals (Figure 10). These intervals can be
thought of as being convergent if they get shorter
and shorter and are contained one in the other.
There are many ways of finding limits in this lattice
as shown in Figure 11. Of course, you need not converge to a perfect element; the upper and lower
limits might never come together.

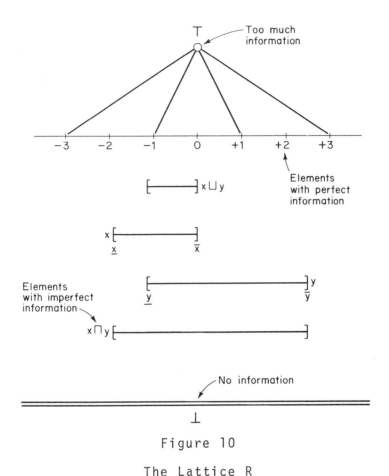

Figure 10

The Lattice R

Speaking more precisely, the intervals

$$x = [\underline{x},\overline{x}]$$

have upper and lower limits $\underline{x}$ and $\overline{x}$. The partial ordering is defined by

$$x \sqsubseteq y \quad \text{if} \quad \underline{x} \leq \underline{y} \leq \overline{y} \leq \overline{x},$$

which means that set-theoretically the interval x contains the interval y. The elements $\perp$ and $\top$ are

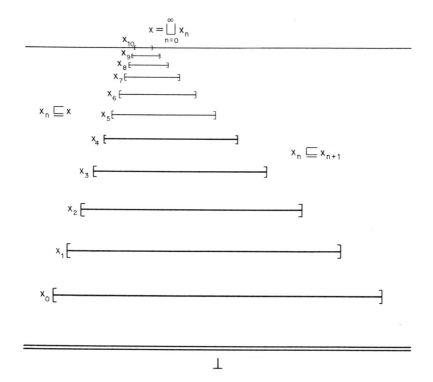

Figure 11

A Limit in R

treated specially; we can take ⊥ as the infinite
interval (no information) and ⊤ as the empty interval
(too much information). This partially ordered set
of intervals forms a lattice. How do you join approximations together? Easy, you take the maximum of
the lower end points and the minimum of the upper
end points. You may be embarrassed to find that
when you do that the resulting interval sometimes
turns out to be empty. For example, if you start
with two disjoint intervals and try to perform this
join, the result is empty. That is just what I
intended by the overdetermined element. Given
inconsistent information about a possible real number (you said it's both supposed to be over here and

over there), then when you try to join all that
information together, there is nothing left to
satisfy the conditions.

*   *   *

Question: *You jump from perfect information
to too much information without any analysis of
degrees of overdeterminance. Why?*

Answer: A good point. My reply to that
question is: If you can think of some way of sorting out degrees of overdeterminance, please do so.
What you should attempt, to make concrete your
analysis of the idea of being overdetermined, is to
fill in this lattice with a system of additional
elements corresponding to the desired degrees. It
will be a quite different lattice, however, and it
may be interesting — if you can think of a clever
construction. I have not thought of a way to do it
yet, but surely a lattice like that must exist.
One additional thought: let the construction be
guided by possible applications.

Question: *What is the need for these intervals?*

Answer: We can see how they behave more clearly
with reference to the graphs of some well-known
functions, to which we now turn.

*   *   *

Figure 12 is a picture of everyone's favorite
function, x^2. Giving an approximate number means
giving upper and lower limits. One might give some
canny guess as to where the value will lie exactly,
but really the only absolute statement that can be
made is that the value lies in a *certain interval*.
Thus the graph determines in the obvious way a
mapping from intervals to intervals. This mapping
is not only monotonic, but it is also continuous
in a lattice sense, which I shall explain presently.

Figure 13 shows the partial function $\sqrt{x}$. For
non-negative intervals, we map as before. For

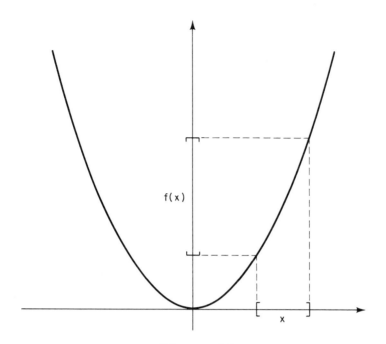

Figure 12

A Function on R

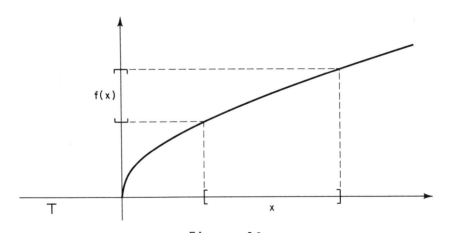

Figure 13

A Function on R

negative intervals the value should be T. (For ambiguous intervals including 0, the value of the function can be that of the restriction of the interval to [0, + ∞).) The reason for doing it this way is that the resulting interval function turns out to be the maximal continuous function (maximal in the sense of the partial ordering ⊑) which agrees with the given point function.

This idea has been used by several people. One place you may not have seen it is in the book by Ramon Moore called *Interval Analysis*.[12] In some reviews of recent papers on interval analysis I saw, the theory was criticized for not being subtle enough for the needs of numerical analysis. The intervals themselves do not give quite enough information about calculation, because one can make some awfully good guesses about where the answers should fall in the middle of the intervals. For example, it may be much more useful to take what is called the centered form. This seems to be a perfectly valid criticism of the utility of the idea in certain numerical calculations, but it is not a criticism of the fact that it is a correct and coherent idea about some features of approximations. Of course, what is disappointing about intervals is how quickly they become too large, how fast you lose information. But that is your fault, not theirs.

Another example of a partial function is 1/x. Look at its graph in Figure 14. If you stay on opposite sides of the singularity, then some good information about the value can be obtained. The only natural way, however, to extend the definition of the function to all intervals is to say that if you inadvertently take an interval which contains zero, then the thing blows up. The value of the function for an interval x containing zero has to be defined ⊥.

A still different example of a partial function is the step function. See Figure 15. If the interval is on one side of the "step," then the value of the function is perfect. If the interval happens to be over on the other side, the value is

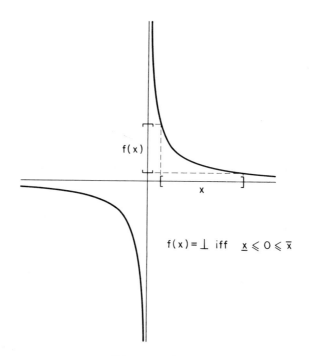

$f(x) = \perp$ iff $\underline{x} \leqslant 0 \leqslant \overline{x}$

Figure 14

A Partial Function

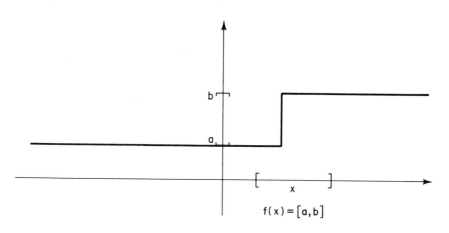

$f(x) = [a,b]$

Figure 15

The Step Function

also perfect. If on the other hand the interval
bridges the step, then you do not know whether you
want the upper or the lower part. So the value of
the function in that case is the whole step.

*   *   *

Question: *If you took the interval [-1, +1]
for 1/x, you still know that f(x) is either larger
than +1 or smaller than -1. So since you have this
information, why do you pick the worst estimate ⊥?*

Answer: I have not been able to settle on the
best way to work this out. There are other kinds
of lattices that would allow you to give information
about numbers where, say, either the number is
between 1 and 2, or the number is between 1000 and
1002 or the number is somewhere else. In other
words, there may be *divided intervals*. A certain
notion of approximation then would apply, and we
would be able to give more clever answers for this
particular function. But you have to change the
underlying lattice to do this. There may be several
different ideas about how approximations work. If
you have an idea, my suggestion is to try to embody
it in a specific mathematical structure like a
lattice and see what happens. One suggestion is to
try the lattice of compact sets which is an expansion of the lattice of closed intervals.

*   *   *

There are two things that I have learned from
these lattices that I want to re-emphasize: first,
the functions that naturally arise are monotonic,
for they preserve the "direction" of the information,
(see Figure 16). That is a very easy conclusion to
arrive at, but these examples from the real numbers
and other domains lead to the same result. The
second, more important conclusion is that computable
functions ought to be continuous. The very abstract
definition of continuity appropriate for a large ·
number of lattices (most of which you will never
want to look at) is that the function should preserve directed least upper bounds (see Figure 17).

Given D, $\sqsubseteq$

    A FUNCTION $F: D \rightarrow D$

IS CALLED MONOTONIC IFF

    $X \sqsubseteq Y$ IMPLIES $F(X) \sqsubseteq F(Y)$,

FOR ALL $X, Y \in D$.

Figure 16

All Computable Functions are Monotonic

Given D, $\sqsubseteq$ AND D', $\sqsubseteq'$

    A FUNCTION $F: D \rightarrow D'$

IS CALLED CONTINUOUS IFF FOR ALL
DIRECTED SUBSETS $X \subseteq D$ WE HAVE

    $F(\bigsqcup X) = \bigsqcup'\{F(X) : X \in X\}$.

Figure 17

All Computable Functions are Continuous

More simply, a generally adequate definition is
the following: Suppose you have a chain of elements
with increasing information. Then the condition
that f be continuous is that f preserve limits, just
as in the definition of the ordinary calculus. We
can write

$$f\left(\bigsqcup_{n=0}^{\infty} x_n\right) = \bigsqcup_{n=0}^{\infty} f(x_n),$$

provided $x_n \sqsubseteq x_{n+1}$ holds for all n.

As a matter of fact, this approach includes the definition of the calculus: because if you think of everywhere defined, continuous point functions they will naturally give you lattice mappings of closed intervals, as we have seen. Saying that you have a limit of intervals is saying something about the limsup and liminf of the lower and upper bounds. Saying that such a limit is preserved is thus really the ordinary definition of continuity. Note, however, that in the lattice formulation there are *many more* continuous functions than there are everywhere defined continuous point functions. I have given you an example of the step function and the functions $\sqrt{x}$ and $1/x$. Both of these satisfy the definition of continuity and can be regarded as partial functions. Therefore the theory of continuous functions that I would like to sell here not only includes *perfect* functions but it **also** includes *partial* functions. And the partial functions that it may include can be very partial indeed, but they are all treated uniformly.

In more abstract terms, given any two complete lattices D and D' we can form the function space [D → D'] of all continuous functions from the first into the second (see Figure 18). For the interval lattice R we have seen several examples of functions in [R → R], and the new idea is to regard these function spaces also as lattices and to define continuous functions on them.

In topology, continuity is defined by neighborhoods in the well-known manner. In these lattices we have used the alternate definition of preservation of limits, but it is helpful to intuition to get some idea of the appropriate neighborhoods in the lattices. We can define open sets in lattice-theoretic terms as follows: A subset $U \subseteq D$ is open if and only if the following conditions are satisfied:

(i)   whenever x ε U and x $\sqsubseteq$ y,
         then y ε U; and

(ii)   whenever $Z \subseteq D$ is directed
and $\bigsqcup Z \; \varepsilon \; \overline{U}$, then $Z \cap U \neq \emptyset$.

Roughly speaking an open set (i) contains along with an element all that it approximates and (ii) only contains a limit if it already contains at least one term of the limit.

As a set $[D \to D']$ is the set of all continuous functions $F : D \to D'$. We define $\sqsubseteq$ on this set by:

$F \sqsubseteq G$ iff $F(x) \sqsubseteq G(x)$, for all $x \; \varepsilon \; D$.

This lattice is complete because we have for $\mathcal{F} \subseteq [D \to D']$

$$(\bigsqcup \mathcal{F})(x) = \bigsqcup \{F(x): F \; \varepsilon \; \mathcal{F}\},$$

for all $x \; \varepsilon \; D$. In this way the operation $F(x)$ of application becomes continuous not only in the variable x, but also in F.

Figure 18

The Lattice $[D \to D']$

In the lattice R an example of an open set would be given by two numbers $a < b$ where we take:

$$U = \{x \; \varepsilon \; R : a < \underline{x} \leq \overline{x} < b\} \quad .$$

As a matter of fact it can be shown that every open set in R is the union of such special open sets (with the convention that $T \; \varepsilon \; U$, $\{T\}$ is open, and D itself is open.)

In the lattice $[R \to R]$ instead of "open" intervals (a,b), we use a kind of generalized step

function to specify the basic neighborhoods of the
space. The picture below should make it clear how
this works (Figure 19). We see a step function
(whose values are always approximate reals) where
a perfect function is shown strictly inside the
step function. The set of all functions (partial
and total) strictly inside forms the neighborhood
in question.

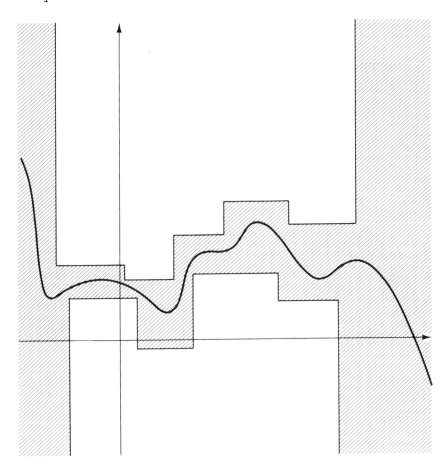

Figure 19

A Generalized Step Function and
its Corresponding Neighborhood

The strict insideness relation can be defined abstractly in any complete lattice:

$$x \prec y \quad \text{iff} \quad y \in \text{Int}\{z \in D : x \sqsubseteq z\} \ ,$$

where Int indicates the topological interior of the set mentioned. What is special about the lattices we have been discussing is that this strict relation is sufficient for approximation. Specifically our lattices satisfy the equation:

$$y = \bigsqcup\{x \in D : x \prec y\} \ ,$$

which is equivalent to the equation:

$$y = \bigsqcup\{\bigsqcap U : y \in U\} \ ,$$

where U ranges over the open subsets of D. (The " $\bigsqcap$ " denotes the greatest lower bound operation in the lattices.) Such complete lattices I call *continuous lattices*. They have a very interesting topological theory, but I have no time to go into details here[13]

The main advantage of studying continuous lattices is that their theory of continuous functions works out so well, and it gives you just what you want. For example, the fixed-point operator, defined mathematically as associating with every continuous function with arguments and values in a lattice D its least fixed point, is indeed a continuous function Y in the space $[[D \to D] \to D]$ (See Figure 20). (What is nice here is that $[D \to D']$ is a continuous lattice if D and D' are.) As another kind of example, we may mention the constructs $D \times D'$ and $D+D'$ on continuous lattices as shown in the Figures 21, 22, and 23. There will be many continuous functions in such spaces as:

$$[[D \times D'] \to D]$$
$$[D \to [D+D']]$$
$$[[D \to [D' \to D'']] \to [[D \times D'] \to D''].$$

This brings us back now to the λ-calculus. We

LET $F : [N \to N] \to [N \to N]$, WHERE

$F(F) = \lambda N.(N=0 \to 0, F(N-1)+2N-1)$.

THEN F IS MONOTONIC AND ALSO CONTINUOUS.

- QUESTION: DOES THERE EXIST A FUNCTION $F \varepsilon [N \to N]$ SUCH THAT $F(F) = F$?

- ANSWER: YES, IN FACT IN THIS EXAMPLE $F = \lambda N.N^2$. BUT WE CAN PROVE IN GEN-ERAL, FOR ANY CONTINUOUS FUNCTION F, THAT A LEAST FIXED POINT IS GIVEN BY:

$$F = \bigsqcup_{M=0}^{\infty} F^M(\bot).$$

THIS METHOD PROVIDES A GENERAL APPROACH TO RECURSION.

Figure 20

An Example

have first the typed calculus of functions where you must say (as we have just been doing) what the domain and range of a function is. To do so we introduce the λ-abstraction operation with a typed variable as shown in the Figures 24 and 25.

But I started out this lecture by talking about the untyped λ-calculus. Strictly speaking the model I want to construct for this theory is not actually untyped, because it has a quite definite set of elements. The point is that in the model the

As a set $[D \times D']$ is the usual
cartesian product of the sets D and D';
that is, the set of all ordered pairs
$\langle x,x' \rangle$ with $x \in D$ and $x' \in D'$. We
define $\sqsubseteq$ on this set for all $x,y \in D$
and $x',y' \in D'$ by:

$\langle x,x' \rangle \sqsubseteq \langle y,y' \rangle$ iff $x \sqsubseteq y$ and $x' \sqsubseteq y'$.

This lattice is complete because
we have for $\maltese \subseteq [D \times D']$:

$\sqcup \maltese = \langle \sqcup X, \sqcup X' \rangle$, where
$X = \{x \in D : \langle x,x' \rangle \in \maltese$, some $x' \in D'\}$
$X' = \{x' \in D' ; \langle x,x' \rangle \in \maltese$, some $x \in D\}$

Figure 21

The Lattice [D x D']

operations of forming f(x) and λx.[...x...] require
no distinction of type since all the elements indicated belong to one and the same domain. The trick
is to form this domain so that the operations
ultimately defined have good properties.

The method of solution I discovered is by the
iteration of the function space construction and by
a final passage to the limit in making at the end
a complete space (complete lattice). The details
are a bit long, but I can sketch for you some of
the essential ideas. Let $D_0 = D$ be any given
(continuous) lattice. Define recursively a sequence
of lattices by the recursion:

As a set $[D + D']$ is just the disjoint union of the two sets D and D' but with the top and bottom elements identified. In pictures we have:

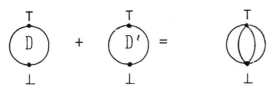

The definitions of the lattice operations on the sum are clear.

● Assumption: We now assume that all lattices considered have isolated tops. This means that if $T = \bigsqcup X$, then $T = \bigsqcup X_0$ for some finite subset $X_0 \subseteq X$.

Figure 22

The Lattice $[D + D']$

$$D_{n+1} = [D_n \to D_n].$$

Thought of in the ordinary way these form a sequence of higher-and higher-type space. Our model is going to be a kind of "completion" of the "union" of these spaces, and if we like we can call it an *infinite type space* D_∞. But we have to be careful just how we take the union.

As it turns out a disjoint union will not do: we must first map each D_n homeomorphically onto a subspace of D_{n+1}. Then we can pretend that

$$D_n \subseteq D_{n+1}$$

IN PICTURES WE HAVE:

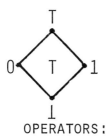

THIS IS THE LATTICE OF TRUTH VALUES, OR BOOLEAN VALUES, 0 AND 1. IT IS USED TOGETHER WITH OTHER LATTICES VIA THESE BASIC OPERATORS:

$$\supset : [T \times D \times D] \to D, \text{ WHERE}$$

$$\supset(T,X,Y) = \begin{cases} X \sqcup Y & \text{IF} \quad T = T \\ X & \text{IF} \quad T = 1 \\ Y & \text{IF} \quad T = 0 \\ \bot & \text{IF} \quad T = \bot \end{cases}$$

$$? : [D + D'] \to T, \text{ WHERE}$$

$$?(Y) = \begin{cases} T & \text{IF} \quad Y = T \\ 0 & \text{IF} \quad \bot \neq L_0(Y) \neq T \\ 1 & \text{IF} \quad \bot \neq L_1(Y) \neq T \\ \bot & \text{IF} \quad Y = \bot \end{cases}$$

Figure 23

The Lattice T

making a union possible. D then is the completion of this union, but when you get down to details it is more easily described as the inverse limit of the spaces D_n. That is a well-known style of construction in algebra and topology, and inverse limits naturally preserve various completeness properties in a highly convenient way. Though I cannot show you the mechanics here, I can at least

SUPPOSE $(\ldots X \ldots)$, WITH VALUES IN D', IS CONTINUOUS IN THE VARIABLE X, WHICH TAKES VALUES IN D. THEN

$$\lambda X: D.(\ldots X \ldots)$$

IS THE λ-EXPRESSION FOR THAT FUNCTION $F \in [D \to D']$ SUCH THAT

$$F(X) = (\ldots X \ldots)$$

FOR ALL $X \in D$.

● THEOREM: IF $(\ldots X \ldots Y \ldots)$, WITH VALUES IN D'', IS CONTINUOUS IN $X \in D$ AND $Y \in D'$, THEN

$$\lambda Y : D'. (\ldots X \ldots Y \ldots),$$

WITH VALUES IN $[D' \to D'']$, IS CONTINUOUS IN X.

● COROLLARY: THE USE OF ITERATED λ-ABSTRACTS IS FULLY JUSTIFIED.

Figure 24

The λ-Notation

show you the mappings we need. For each pair of spaces D_n and D_{n+1} there will be two mappings

$$i_n : D_n \to D_{n+1} \text{ , and}$$

$$j_n : D_{n+1} \to D_n \text{ ,}$$

where i_n will be an injection and j_n will be a kind of projection. At stage 0, we let $i_0(x)$ be the constant function with value x, which is an element

SOME IMPORTANT λ-ABSTRACTS

$I : D \to D$, WHERE

$\qquad I = \lambda x : D. \; x$

$K : D \to [D' \to D]$, WHERE

$\qquad K = \lambda x : D. \; \lambda y : D'. \; x$

$S : [D \to [D' \to D'']] \to [[D \to D'] \to [D \to D'']]$

$\qquad S = \lambda F. \lambda G. \lambda x. \; F(x)(G(x))$

(NOTE: HERE THE RESTRICTIONS ON THE VARIABLES ARE UNDERSTOOD.)

THE FIXED POINT OPERATOR

$Y : [D \to D] \to D$, WHERE

$\qquad Y(F)$ = THE LEAST FIXED POINT OF THE FUNCTION F.

(NOTE: IT MUST BE PROVED THAT Y IS INDEED CONTINUOUS.)

Figure 25

of the function space $D_1 = [D_0 \to D_0]$. Together with this we let $j_0(f) = F(\bot)$; in other words to each function in D_1 we associate its minimum value. Next we define at higher types:

$$i_{n+1} = \lambda x : D_n \; . \; i_n \circ x \circ j_n, \text{ and}$$

$$j_{n+1} = \lambda y : D_{n+1} \; . \; j_n \circ y \circ i_n \; ,$$

where $\circ$ denotes functional composition. Though I

cannot indicate just why to you now, these definitions allow the function spaces to fit inside one
another in a very satisfactory way.

The surprise, to me at least, was that by
passing to the limit space D_∞ it happens that

$$D_\infty = [D_\infty \rightarrow D_\infty] ,$$

or more rigorously speaking: these spaces are
homeomorphic, even isomorphic as lattices.   The
whole secret of course was to use continuous functions throughout. Mathematically the theory is very
"smooth," but intuitively there is considerable
justification in saying that all functions (all
practical functions, all computable functions) are
continuous. What my theory contributes is just the
right kind of flexible meaning to the word "continuous."

In other publications I have shown how this
approach can be adapted to syntax and semantics for
various languages[1,4] In my last slide I just want to
indicate that the iterative construction of the
space D_∞ can be used for an extensive variety of
other spaces (Figure 26). We can think of these
spaces as recursively defined data types on which
I have found a way of imposing a very useful
topology. These "equations" read very much like
BNF syntactical definitions, but we must remember
that I am constructing *spaces* not sets of expressions. What fascinates me are the limit points to
be found in these spaces, and I hope that I have
been able in this lecture to convey some of the
fascination to you.

- THE INTEGERS
  $$N = 1 + N$$
- LIST STRUCTURES OVER D
  $$V = D + [V \times V]$$
- A SPACE OF "PATHS" OVER D
  $$V = D + [V + V]$$
- A λ-CALCULUS MODEL OVER D
  $$V = D + [V \rightarrow V]$$
- A UNIVERSAL DOMAIN OVER D
  $$V = D + [V + V] + [V \times V] + [V \rightarrow V]$$

- A LATTICE OF "EXPRESSIONS"
  $$E = A + [E \times E] + [E \times E]$$
- A PURE λ-CALCULUS MODEL
  $$V = [V \rightarrow V], \text{ WHERE}$$
  $$D = \{\{x \in V : x = K(x)\}\}$$

Figure 26

Recursively Defined Data Types

NOTES AND REFERENCES

1.   The mathematical ideas sketched in this lecture
grew out of joint work with Christopher Strachey on
semantics for programming languages begun in the
fall of 1969 in Oxford. The presentation here was
illustrated by slides most of which the editor gen-
erously had redrawn for inclusion in the printed
text. There was not time in the lecture to enter
too deeply into the semantical applications, but
further information can be found in the following
publications, sequels to which are in active prepar-
ation:

> Dana Scott,"The Lattice of Flow Diagrams,"
> *Semantics of Algorithmic Languages*, E.
> Engeler ed., Springer Lecture Notes in
> Mathematics, Vol. 188, 1971, 311-366.

> Dana Scott and Christopher Strachey,
> "Toward a Mathematical Semantics for Com-
> puter Languages," *1971 Symposium on Com-
> puters and Automata*, Microwave Research
> Institute Proceedings, Vol. 21, Polytech-
> nic Institute of Brooklyn, in press.

The original announcement of the work is to be
found in:

> Dana Scott, "Outline of a Mathematical
> Theory of Computation," *Proc*. *of the
> Fourth Annual Princeton Conference on
> Information Sciences and Systems*, 1970.

2.   Church's final publication on the λ-calculus
was:

> A. Church, *The Calculi of Lambda-Con-
> version*, Annals of Mathematics Studies,
> Vol. 6, 2nd ed., Princeton 1951.

in which references to earlier work of his and his
students can be found. Additional references are
of course to be found in:

> H.B. Curry and Robert Feys, *Combinatory Logic*, Vol. 1, Amsterdam, 1958. (Vol. 2 is in press.)

3. The work of Curry and his collaborators references in 2. gives the most up-to-date information.

4. References can be found in:

> T.B. Steel, Jr., ed., *Formal Language Description Languages for Computer Programming*, Amsterdam 1966.

5. Cf. the paper and references in Peter Wegner's contribution to this volume; some more recent developments can be found in

> Christopher Wadsworth, "Semantics and Pragmatics of the λ-Calculus," D.Phil. Thesis, Oxford University, September 1971.

6. The paper has only appeared in Italian:

> Corrado Boehm, "Alcune Proprieta Della Forme β-η-Normali Del λ-κ-Calcolo," *Pubblicazioni dell'Instituto per le Applicazioni Del Calcolo*, No. 696, Consiglio Nazionale Delle Ricerche, Roma 1968.

but an outline of the proof is given Curry, op.cit, Vol. 2. Related work can be found in the thesis of Wadsworth (note 5) and in:

> H.P. Barendregt, "Some Extensional Term Models for Combinatory Logics and λ-Calculi," Thesis, Utrecht 1971.

This paper also contains valuable further references.

7. The paradoxical combinator is explained in Curry, op.cit., pp. 177 ff.

8. The proof which has as yet not appeared in print, was found by Park in early 1970.

9. This example is taken from:

> Corrado Boehm, "The CUCH as a Formal and Description Language," in T.B. Steel, ed. (cf. Note 4), 179-197.

See especially page 183 f, and page 195 f.

10. An interesting recent survey of "classical" lattice theory can be found in:

> J.C. Abbott, ed., *Trends in Lattice Theory*, Van Nostrand Reinhold Mathematical Studies, Vol. 31, New York - London, 1970.

But as far as the author can judge, none of the applications mentioned in that book point in the direction needed for the present study.

11. A topological explanation of the use of lattices and the connection with extension properties of functions is given in:

> Dana Scott, "Continuous Lattices," *Proc. Dalhousie Conference*, Springer Lecture Notes, in press.

12. The exact reference is:

> Ramon E. Moore, *Interval Analysis*, Prentice-Hall, 1966.

Note, however, that Moore does not use $\bot$ and $\top$ and does not have a lattice. Also he did not at that time see that the ideas could be extended to other structures. From the point of view of recursive function theory the following references are relevant:

> Daniel Lacombe, "Extension de la Notion de Fonction Récursive aux Functions d'une ou Plusieurs Variables Réeles I, II, III." *Comptes Rendus*, Vol. 240, 1955, 2478-80; Vol. 241, 1955, 13-14; Vol. 241, 1955, 151-153.

————, "Remarques Sur les Opérateurs Récursifs et sur les Function Récursives d'une Variable Réele," Ibid, Vol. 241, 1955, 1250-52.

Martin Davis, "Computable Functionals of Arbitrary Finite Type," *Constructivity in Mathematics*, A. Heyting, ed., North Holland, 1959, 281-284.

A. Nerode, "Some Stone Spaces and Recursion Theory," *Duke Mathematical Journal*, Vol. 26, 1959, 397-406.

Richard Platek, "Foundations of Recursion Theory," Stanford Ph.D. Thesis, 1965, unpublished.

The author learned about the use of partial orderings in function spaces from the last reference. It was only recently, however, that he saw how to tie together all of these ideas with the aid of topology as explained in "Continuous Lattices"(see note 11). More attention has to be given to the recursion-theoretic aspects of these spaces, however.

13. See the reference of note 11.

14. See the references of note 1.

A CORRECTNESS PROOF USING RECURSIVELY DEFINED FUNCTIONS

J. H. Morris, Jr.
University of California, Berkeley

This paper presents a rigorous correctness proof for the Fisher-Galler method of recording equivalence relations [1]. It is of interest because (1) the proof illustrates the use of truncation induction as described in [2], (2) the program involves a subroutine and the non-trivial use of pointers, and (3) the proof illustrates how translating programs into functional form can be useful.

THE PROBLEM

The objective is to keep track of an arbitrary equivalence relation over a finite set of integers $\{1,2,\ldots,k\}$. We must provide two subroutines Enter, and Equiv. After initialization Enter may be called with pairs of integers in the range [1,k] and is expected to record the fact that they are equivalent. Equiv(x,y) should return *true* if x and y are equivalent -- either because Enter(x,y) has been executed previously or because the laws of reflexivity, symmetry, or transitivity make them so, given other explicit equivalences. Otherwise Equiv returns *false*.

THE SCHEME

The Fisher-Galler scheme for doing this is described in [1, p. 353] and works as follows:

Initially, an array A[1:k] is set to all zeros. Now define the subroutine Rep(x) by the flow-chart

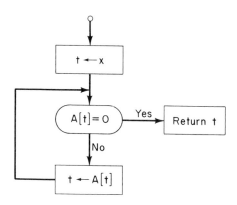

Rep(x) is intended to return a canonical Representative of x's equivalence class. Initially, Rep(x) = x for 1 < x < k. The value of Equiv(x,y) is *true* if Rep(x) = Rep(y) and *false* otherwise. The routine Enter(x,y) is defined by

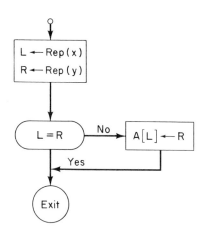

FORMALIZATION OF CORRECTNESS

To formulate the correctness of this scheme we consider a sequence of pairs $<\ell_1,\gamma_1>,\ldots,<\ell_N,\gamma_N>$ which Enter might be called with and which form the basis for the equivalence relation. Specifically, define the equivalence relation as the least relation, E, such that

(1) $E(x,x)$, for all $1 \le x \le k$
(2) $E(\ell_i,\gamma_i)$, for $1 \le \overline{i} \le \overline{N}$

(3)   If $E(x,y)$ then $E(y,x)$
(4)   If $E(x,y)$ and $E(y,z)$ then $E(x,z)$

Then the correctness condition is: after Enter(ℓ_i,γ_i) has been executed for $i = 1,\ldots,N$ then Equiv(x,y) = *true* iff $E(x,y)$. Naturally it is assumed that $1 \le \ell_i, \gamma_i \le k$ for $1 \le i \le N$.

TRANSFORMATION TO FUNCTIONAL PROGRAMS

We shall define two functions Rep and Enter corresponding to the programs in the definition of the Fisher-Galler scheme.

The array A will itself be represented by a series of functions; instead of assigning to its elements we produce a new function, differing from the old for one argument.

Rep$(x,A) \triangleq A(x) \simeq 0 \rightarrow x;$ Rep $(A(x),A)$

Enter$(x,y,A) \triangleq$ *let* $L = $ Rep(x,A)
  and $R = $ Rep(y,A)
  in $L \simeq R \rightarrow A;$

which is equivalent to $[\lambda z. \ z \simeq L \rightarrow R; \ A(x)]$

The notation used is approximately that of PAL [3]. See the Appendix for a summary of the notation.

The definition of Rep should not cause difficulty for anyone familiar with recursive definitions and their relationship to looping programs. Enter however, merits some explanation. Intuitively, the value of Enter(x,y,A) is a function describing the contents of the array in terms of x,y, and A which itself is a function describing the contents of the array before Enter(x,y) (the imperative version) is executed. The definition of Enter says that

(1)   The array is unchanged if Rep(x,A) = Rep(y,A). Otherwise, (2) the array differs from the old one only at the element with subscript Rep(x,A) where its new value is Rep(y,A). The λ-expression

$$\lambda z.\ z \simeq L \rightarrow R;\ A(z)$$

describes just such a function, given the local definitions of L and R.

Notice that the finiteness of the array is no longer a consideration; Enter and Rep will work properly for any arguments other than 0 rather than just those in the range [1,k]. Thus the result we shall prove is slightly more general than that required.

To describe the state of the array after i pairs have been Enter'ed we define

$$M(i) \triangleq i \simeq 0 \rightarrow [\lambda j.\ 0];$$
$$\text{Enter } (\ell_i, \gamma_i, M(i-1))$$

Thus if no pairs have been entered M(i) = M(0), the array all of whose elements are zero. Otherwise it is the array produced by Entering the pair $<\ell_i, \gamma_i>$ to the array M(i-1).

The correctness problem can now be succinctly stated as

Theorem   E(x,y) iff Rep(x,M(N)) = Rep(y,M(N))

It requires a certain amount of insight and facility with recursive definitions to transform programs in the way done here. Although there are completely mechanical ways of translating imperative programs into functional ones, it is unlikely that they would produce exactly the definitions above.

The reader may feel that the original problem has been transformed beyond recognition, so we shall endeavor to relate the ensuing proof of the theorem to the original programs as we go along.

THE PROOF OF THE THEOREM

The method of *truncation induction* will be used heavily in what follows. Briefly, it says that if a function, f is defined by

$$f(x) \triangleq E[f,x]$$

then any statement about its truncations, f_i, of the form

$$(\forall_i) \; [f_i(x) \neq \omega \; => \rho(x,f_i(x))]$$

implies the corresponding statement about f. Here $f_i(x) = $ means $f_i(x)$ is undefined, and the truncations are defined by

$$f_0(x) \triangleq \omega$$
$$f_{i+1}(x) \triangleq E[f_i,x]$$

The method is presented and discussed more fully in [2].

The proof consists of seven lemmas. We assume throughout that

$$1 \leq i \leq N, \; \ell_i \neq 0, \; \gamma_i \neq 0, \; x \neq 0 \text{ and } y \neq 0 \; .$$

Lemma 1. If $x \neq 0$ and $Rep_j(x,A) = C \neq \omega$

then $c \neq 0$ and $A(C) = 0$.

(I.e., if Rep(x,A) halts before traversing the loop j times, then its value is not zero but A applied to its value is zero.)

Proof: By induction on j. Assume the Lemma for j and suppose

$$x \neq 0 \;\Delta\; Rep_{j+1}(x,A) = C \neq \omega$$

Then either

(i) $A(x) = 0 \;\Delta\; C = x$ which implies $C \neq 0$ and
$A(C) = 0$

or   (ii) $A(x) \neq 0 \;\Delta\; f_j(A(x),A) = C \neq \omega$ which implies
$C \neq 0$ and $A(C) = 0$ by the induction hypothesis.

Since the Lemma is vacuously true for j = 0 it is true for all j.

QED.

Lemma 2. $Rep(x,M(i)) \neq \omega$.

(I.e., Rep always halts if the array has been produced by Entering i pairs to an initially zeroed array.)

Proof: The proof proceeds by two nested induction arguments. The base of the outer induction,

$$Rep(x,M(0)) \neq \omega$$

is obvious so assume, for fixed i, and all x

$$Rep(x,M(i)) \neq \omega \tag{2.1}$$

Now, to show $Rep(x,M(i+1)) \neq \omega$ we prove

$$Rep_j(x,M(i)) \neq \omega =>Rep(x,M(i+1)) \neq \omega \tag{2.2}$$

by induction on j. The case j = 0 is vacuously true, so assume (2.2) for fixed j and all x and assume

$$Rep_{j+1}(y,M(i)) \neq \omega \qquad (2.3)$$

for a particular y.

Let L = Rep(ℓ_{i+1},M(i)) and R = Rep(γ_{i+1}M(i)); neither one can be ω by (2.1).

Case 1: L = R

$$M(i+1) = Enter (\ell_{i+1},\gamma_{i+1},M(i)) = M(i)$$

so Rep(y,M(i+1)) = Rep(y,M(i)) $\neq \omega$ by (2.1).

Case 2: y = L $\neq$ R

$$M(i+1)(y) = [\lambda z. \ z \simeq L \to R; \ M(i)(z)](y)$$

$$= y \simeq L \to R; \ M(i)(R)$$

$$= R \neq 0 \qquad \text{(by Lemma 1.)}$$

Thus

$$Rep(y,M(i+1)) = Rep(R,M(i+1))$$

But

$$M(i+1)(R) = M(i)(R) \qquad \text{since } R \neq L$$

$$= 0 \qquad \text{(by Lemma 1.)}$$

Hence

$$Rep(y,M(i+1)) = R \neq \omega \qquad \text{(by (2.1))}$$

Case 3: y $\neq$ L, L $\neq$ R

$$M(i+1)(y) = M(i)(y)$$

Case 3.1: $M(i)(y) = 0$
Then $Rep(y,M(i+1)) = y \neq \omega$

Case 3.2: $M(i)(y) \neq 0$
Then $Rep(y,M(i+1)) = Rep(M(i)(y),M(i+1))$

Also $Rep_{j+1}(y,M(i)) = Rep_j(M(i)(y),M(i))$

$$\neq \omega \qquad \text{(By (2.3))}$$

Hence $Rep(M(i)(y),M(i+1)) \neq \omega$ (By (2.2))

so $Rep(y,M(i+1)) \neq \omega$

The three cases establish (2.2) for all j. Then we have

$$Rep(x,M(i)) \neq \omega \Rightarrow (\exists j)[Rep_j(x,M(i)) \neq \omega]$$

$$\Rightarrow Rep(x,M(i+1)) \neq \omega$$

$$\text{(By (2.2))}$$

which establishes the induction step of the outer induction.

$$\text{QED.}$$

Lemma 3.

$$Rep(x,M(i+1)) = Rep(x,M(i)) \simeq Rep(\ell_{i+1},M(i))$$

$$\rightarrow Rep(\gamma_{i+1},M(i));$$

$$Rep(x,M(i)) \qquad\qquad (3.1)$$

(I.e., after Entering the pair $<\ell_{i+1},\gamma_{i+1}>$ in the array the value of Rep depends upon the old array as indicated by the right-hand side.)

Proof: Let L and R be defined as in Lemma 2 and define

$$X = Rep(x,M(i))$$

then the right-hand side of (3.1) is

$$X \simeq L \to R; \; X$$

The Lemma will follow from proving

$$Rep_j(x, M(i+1)) = c \neq \omega \Rightarrow c = (X \simeq L \to R; \; X)$$

$$(3.2)$$

Assume (3.2) for fixed j and suppose

$$Rep_{j+1}(x, M(i+1)) = c \neq \omega \qquad (3.3)$$

Case 1: $L = R$

   Then $M(i+1) = M(i)$ so $c = Rep_{j+1}(x, M(i)) = X$

   But $(X \simeq L \to R; \; X) = (X \simeq L \to X; \; X)$

$$= X$$

Case 2: $X = L \neq R$

   Then $(X \simeq L \to R; \; X) = R$

   Case 2.1: $x = L$

      Then $M(i+1)(x) = R \neq 0$ (By Lemma 1)

      so $Rep_{j+1}(x, M(i+1)) = Rep_j(R, M(i+1))$

      Now $M(i+1)(R) = (R \simeq L \to R; \; M(i)(R))$

$$= M(i)(R) \qquad \text{(since } L \neq R)$$

$$= 0 \qquad \text{(By Lemma 1)}$$

      Hence $Rep_j(R, M(i+1)) = R$

      So $Rep_{j+1}(x, M(i+1)) = R$

   Case 2.2: $x \neq L$

      Then $M(i+1)(x) = M(i)(x)$

$$\neq 0 \text{ , (for } M(i)(x) = 0 \text{ implies}$$

$$x = X = L)$$

so $Rep_{j+1}(x, M(i+1)) =$

$\qquad Rep_{j}(M(i)(x), M(i+1)) \neq \omega \qquad$ (By (3.3))

By (3.2), the induction hypothesis,

$\qquad Rep_{j}(M9i)(x), M(i+1)) =$

$\qquad Rep(M(i)(x), M(i)) \simeq L \rightarrow R;$

$\qquad Rep(M(i)(x), M(i))$

$\qquad = X \simeq L \rightarrow R; \ X$

$\qquad = R$

Case 3: $\ X \neq L \neq R$

Then $(X \simeq L \rightarrow R; \ X) = X$

Now $x \neq L$, otherwise we would have $X = L$.

so $\ M(i+1)(x) = M(i)(x)$

Case 3.a: $\ M(i)(X) = 0$

$\qquad$ Then $\ Rep_{j+1}(x, M(i+1)) = x$

$\qquad$ and $\ X = Rep(x, M(i)) = x$

Case 3.b: $\ M(i)(x) \neq 0$

$\qquad$ Then $Rep_{j+1}(x, M(i+1)) =$

$\qquad\qquad Rep_{j}(M(i)(x), M(i+1)) \neq \omega \qquad$ (By (3.3))

$\qquad$ By (3.2), the induction hypothesis,

$$\text{Rep}_j(M(i)(x),M(i+1)) =$$

$$\text{Rep}(M(i)(x),M(i)) \simeq L \rightarrow R;$$

$$\text{Rep}(M(i)(x),M(i))$$

$$= (X \simeq L \rightarrow R; X) = X$$

This completes the proof of 3.2 for all j by induction. By the principle of truncation induction we may drop the j from 3.2. By Lemma 2, $\text{Rep}(x,M(i+1)) \neq \omega$ so 3.2 implies the Lemma.

QED.

Lemma 4: $E(x,\text{Rep}(x,M(i)))$ (4.1)

(I.e., Rep maps x into an equivalent element)

Proof: (By induction in i)

If $i = 0$ (4.1) is $E(x,x)$

Suppose (4.1) is true for fixed i.

Case 1: $\text{Rep}(x,M(i)) = \text{Rep}(\ell_{i+1},M(i))$

Then $\text{Rep}(x,M(i+1)) = \text{Rep}(\gamma_{i+1},M(i))$

(By Lemma 3)

Now (4.1) implies

$$E(x,\text{Rep}(\ell_{i+1},M(i)) \quad ,$$

$$E(\ell_{i+1},\text{Rep}(\ell_{i+1},M(i))) \quad ,$$

and $E(\gamma_{i+1},\text{Rep}(x,M(i+1)))$

By definition

$$E(\ell_{i+1},\gamma_{i+1})$$

so $E(x, \text{Rep}(x, M(i+1)))$ follows by the transitivity and symmetry of E.

Case 2: $\text{Rep}(x, M(i)) \neq \text{Rep}(\ell_{i+1}, M(i))$

Then $\text{Rep}(x, M(i+1)) = \text{Rep}(x, M(ii))$ (By Lemma 3)

so $(x, \text{Rep}(x, M(i+1)))$ follows from 4.1.

                                                        QED.

Lemma 5: $\text{Rep}(x, M(i)) = \text{Rep}(y, M(i)) \Rightarrow E(x, y)$

(I.e., the scheme does not err by reporting non-equivalent pairs equivalent)

Proof: By Lemma 4 and the transitivity and symmetry of E.

                                                        QED.

Lemma 6: $1 \leq k \leq i \Rightarrow \text{Rep}(\ell_k, M(i)) = \text{Rep}(\gamma_k, M(i))$

                                            (6.1)

(I.e., Enter successfully records all the explicit equivalences)

Proof: By induction on i

For $i = 0$ (6.1) is vacuously true.

Suppose (6.1) is true for fixed i.

Case 1: $1 \leq k \leq i$

$$\text{Rep}(\ell_k, M(i+1)) = \text{Rep}(\ell_k, M(i)) \simeq \text{Rep}(\ell i+1, M(i))$$

$$\text{Rep}(\gamma_{i+1}, M(i)); \qquad\qquad (6.2)$$

$$\text{Rep}(\ell_k, M(i))$$

$$\text{Rep}(\gamma_k, M(i+1)) = \text{Rep}(\gamma_k, M(i)) \simeq \text{Rep}(\ell_{i+1}, M(i))$$

$$\rightarrow \text{Rep}(\gamma_{i+1}, M(i));$$

$$\text{Rep}(\gamma_k, M(i)) \qquad\qquad (6.3)$$

(By Lemma 3)

By (6.1), the induction hypothesis,

$$\text{Rep}(\ell_k, M(i)) = \text{Rep}(\gamma_k, M(i))$$

so the right-hand sides of (6.2) and (6.3) must be equal in either case.

Case 2: $k = i+1$

Then $\text{Rep}(\ell_{i+1}, M(i+1)) = \text{Rep}(\gamma_{i+1}, M(i))$

$$= \text{Rep}(\gamma_{i+1}, M(i+1))$$

(By Lemma 3)

QED.

Lemma 7: $E(x,y) \Rightarrow \text{Rep}(x, M(N)) = \text{Rep}(y, M(N))$

(I.e., the scheme reports all equivalent pairs so)

Proof: The predicate E can be viewed as the "limit" of the following series of "truncated" predicates:

$$E_0 = \{<x,y> \mid x = y \lor x = \ell_i \land y = \gamma_i \land 1 \leq i \leq N\}$$

$E_{i+1} = E_i \cup \{<x,y> \mid E_i(y,x) \; \nabla \; E_i(x,z) \; \Delta \; E_i(z,y)$

для some $z\}$

Thus $E(x,y) \Rightarrow E_i(x,y)$ for some i.

Now we need only prove

$E_i(x,y) \Rightarrow Rep(x,M(N)) = Rep(y,M(N))$ (7.1)

by induction on i.

For i = 0 $E_0(x,y) \Rightarrow x = y$

or $x = \ell_i \; \wedge \; \gamma = \ell_i \; \wedge \; \gamma = \ell_i$

by definition or Lemma 6, respectively.

Suppose $E_{i+1}(x,y)$ and not $E_i(x,y)$ then either

(a) $E_i(y,x)$

or   (b) $E_i(x,z) \wedge E_i(z,y)$ for some z.

In either case $Rep(x,M(N)) = Rep(y,M(N))$ follows from the induction hypothesis and the transitivity and symmetry of = .

                                   QED.

Lemmas 5 and 7 prove the Theorem of section E.

DISCUSSION

The keystone of the foregoing proof is Lemma 3 which describes the behavior of $Rep(x,M(i+1))$ purely in terms of the values of

$Rep(x,M(i))$, $Rep(\ell_{i+1},M(i))$ and $Rep(\gamma_{i+1},M(i))$.

Thus, it allows us to perform induction on the number of pairs Entered in the later lemmas.

Regarding the advantage of transforming the program into functions, my first observation is that I can't think of an easier way to simply state the correctness condition, and the various lemmas.

This ease depends upon the fact that all the expressions we deal with are timeless in the sense that they denote the same value irrespective of any sequence of computations. For example, consider the definition of Enter on page 3. The computation it calls for (by a PAL interpreter, say) is

   1.   Computer Rep(x,A) and Rep(y,A), setting
        L and R to their values.

   2.   If L = R return the function A unaltered.

   3.   Otherwise, return a function A' which,
        when called, will return R if the
        argument is L, otherwise the value of
        A for the argument.

On the other hand, since Rep(x,A) and Rep(y,A) denote the same values regardless of when they are computed we can rewrite Enter as

Enter' (x,y,A) $\triangleq$

   [λz. Rep(x,A) $\simeq$ Rep(y,A) $\rightarrow$ A(z);

        z $\simeq$ Rep(x,A) $\rightarrow$ Rep(y,A);

   A(z)]

This function calls for an entirely different sequence of computations. To compute Enter'(x,y,A) simply return a function A', which, when called with z,

   1.   Computes Rep(x,A) and Rep(y,A) and
        compares their values. If they are
        equal, it returns A(z).

   2.   If they are not equal, Rep(x,A) is
        computed again and compared with z.

If the values are equal, Rep(y,A)
is computed and its value returned.

3.   Otherwise the value of A at z is
     returned.

In a proper implementation of PAL these two
functions will always behave qualitatively the
same. Treating the programs as functions depends
upon this implicit assumption.

Throughout the foregoing proof I was able to
think of expressions like Rep(x,A) in terms of the
objects they denote rather than something to be
evaluated by an interpreter. This "algebraic"
approach seems much more natural.

My second observation is to point out an
implicit assumption introduced by the transformation
to functions: There will be no unexpected side-
effects (i.e., hidden assignments). This applies
not only to the computations of Enter and Rep but
also to any intervening computations not mentioned
in the discussion. For example, if Enter and Rep
are being used in conjunction with some other
programs which happen to assign values to the
vector A the foregoing proof guarantees nothing.
To use this proof to prove something about a larger
program that calls Enter and Rep one must prove that
the array A is left undisturbed or, after writing
the whole program as a function, that Rep and Enter
are always called with previous values of Enter.

This point brings out a more general problem
about correctness proofs: Before they can approach
practical applications we must have ways of combining proofs about sub-programs into proofs about
larger programs without having to reprove everything. How to do this is not clear but practical
experience with debugging offers some hints; e.g.,
hidden side-effects lead to disaster.

One of the goals of this work is to discover
what principles there might be for the design of
programming languages. Specifically, I propose to

moderate the traditional question "How easy is it to write a program to do X?" to be "How easy is it to write and *prove correct* a program to do X?"   In the end, of course, this criterion is just as subjective as the first; but it emphasizes what I feel is an important attribute of a language.

REFERENCES

[1]   Knuth, D.E., *The Art of Computer Programming*, Addison-Wesley, 1968.

[2]   Morris, J.H., "Another Recursion Induction Principle," *Comm. ACM*, May 1971.

[3]   Evans, A., "PAL - A Reference Manual and a Primer," *MIT Department of Electrical Engineering Report*, 1969.

[4]   McCarthy, J., "A Basis of a Mathematical Theory of Computation," *Computer Programming and Formal Systems*, Broffort and Hirsberg (Eds.), Noth-Holland, 1963.

[5]   Floyd, R.W., "Assigning Meanings to Programs," Proceedings of Symposium in Applied Mathematics, *AMS Vol. 19*, 1967.

[6]   Landin, P.J., "The Mechanical Evaluation of Expressions," *Computer Journal 6*, No. 4, 1964.

PAL Notation

All expressions in PAL denote things, either numbers or functions.

$[\lambda z.\ E]$ denotes a function — that function of z which E is. To apply it to an argument, A, one substitutes A for z throughout E and then evaluates the reconstituted E.

f(x)(y) is a multiple functional application denoting the value of f(x) (which is presumably a function) applied to y. If $x = \omega$ or $y = \omega$ the whole expression equals ω.

One may write functions explicitly as in $[\lambda z.\ z+1]$ (2) which has a value of 3.

A conditional expression $E_1 \simeq E_2 \rightarrow A;\ B$ has value A if $E_1 = E_2 \neq \omega$, has value B if $E_1 \neq \omega$, $E_2 \neq \omega$, $E_1 = E_2$, and has value ω if $E_1 = \omega$ or $E_2 = \omega$.

The expression *let* $A = E_1$ *and* $B = E_2$ *in* E_3 is equivalent to $[\lambda (A,B).\ E_3]\ (E_1,E_2)$ which is evaluated by substituting the values of E_1 and E_2 for A and B in E_3 and then evaluating E_3. *let* expressions can thus be thought of as initializing declarations.

A statement like $f(x) \overset{\Delta}{=} E$ is definition and defines the function f to be the "least" function satisfying the equation $f(x) = E$. A more careful discussion of definitions may be found in [Mo].

A CORRECTNESS PROOF OF THE FISHER-GALLER ALGORITHM USING INDUCTIVE ASSERTIONS

Ralph L. London
University of Wisconsin

This paper presents a rigorous correctness proof for the Fisher-Galler algorithm of recording equivalence relations using the method of inductive assertions.

INTRODUCTION

In Morris (1970b), J. H. Morris uses truncation induction (Morris 1970a) to give a correctness proof for the Fisher-Galler algorithm of recording equivalence relations (Knuth 1968, pp. 353-355). When Morris presented his proof at the Symposium, he remarked that he had been unable, after a brief attempt, to give a proof by inductive assertions. Accordingly, the purpose of this note is to record a proof for the algorithm using inductive assertions. The proof will follow the style of London (1970b) and, in addition, will use backward substitution, briefly described in London (1970a). Some comments about Morris' and my proof are also given at the end.

THE AIM OF THE ALGORITHM

The Fisher-Galler algorithm "is to keep track
of an arbitrary equivalence relation over a finite
set of integers [1,k]. We must provide two subroutines, Enter and Equiv. After initialization
Enter may be called with pairs of integers in the
range [1,k] and is expected to record the fact that
they are equivalent. Equiv(x,y) should return *true*
if x and y are equivalent — either because
Enter(x,y) has been executed previously or because
the laws of reflexivity, symmetry, or transitivity
make them so, given other explicit equivalences.
Otherwise Equiv returns *false*." (Morris 1970b,
see Discussion.)

The Fisher-Galler algorithm starts with an
array A[1:k] set to all zeros. A subroutine Rep(x)
is defined (see below), intended to return a
canonical *Rep*resentative of x's equivalence class.
Initially, Rep(x) = x for 1<x<k. The value of
Equiv(x,y) is *true* if Rep(x) = Rep(y) and *false*
otherwise. The subroutine Enter, which uses Rep
twice, is defined below. If ≡ denotes the equivalence relation, the correctness statement is: After
each call of Enter(x,y), then z ≡ w iff Equiv(z,w).

Informally (and not part of the proof), the
array A is viewed as a forest of trees. Rep(x) is,
in fact, the root of the (unique) tree containing
x. Initially the array consists solely of roots
(hence Rep(x) = x). Enter(x,y) makes x and y equivalent by making x's tree into a subtree of the
root of y's tree.

THE RIGOROUS PROOF OF CORRECTNESS

All inputs are assumed to be positive integers
and the array A is initially zeros. It is easy to
verify, therefore, that all quantities manipulated
by the subroutines are non-negative integers. Part
of this verification is omitted.

Lemma 1:   The integer-valued subroutine Rep(x)
is defined by the following flowchart.   If x ≠ 0
and A is a forest on entry to Rep(x) and if (A1)
and (A2) below hold for root (x), then on exit the
returned value t of Rep(x) satisfies

$$0 \neq t = \text{root}(x) \wedge A[t] = 0 \quad .$$

Proof:

Rep(x):

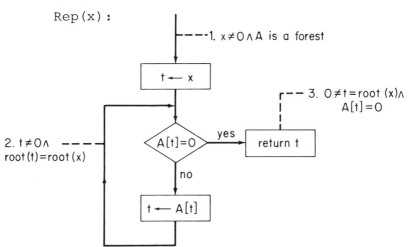

First note a global property of Rep(x), namely
A is unaltered by Rep(x) since only   t   is changed.
Second, we assume for a forest A that if x ≠ 0 then

root (x) = root (A[x])   if   A[x] ≠ 0   (A1)
root (x) = x   if   A[x] = 0.   (A2)

(This property will be shown to hold initially as
part of the proof of Theorem 1.   The property will
be shown to be preserved as part of the proof of
lemma 2 for Enter, the only place where the array
A is changed.)

The assertions are verified by backward substitution: (→ is used for "implies.")

Path 1-3: verification condition (vc):
    x≠0 ∧ A is a forest ∧ A[x]=0
        → 0≠x=root(x) ∧ A[x]=0.
    True by (A2) and identities.

Path 2-3: vc:
    t≠0 ∧ root(t)=root(x) ∧ A[t]=0
        → 0≠t=root(x) ∧ A[t]=0.
    Use (A2) to obtain t = root(t).

Path 1-2: vc:
    x≠0 ∧ A is a forest ∧ A[x]≠0
        → A[x]≠0 ∧ root(A[x])=root(x).
    True by (A1).

Path 2-2: vc:
    t≠0 ∧ root(t)=root(x) ∧ A[t]≠0
        → A[t]≠0 ∧ root(A[t])=root(x).
    Use (A1) to obtain root(t) = root(A[t]).

Since the array is defined only for $A[1:k]$, one should show all array references are in bounds. Since $t≠0$ and t is a non-negative integer, one need only show $t<k$. If we augment assertion 1 (i.e. the assumptions of lemma 1) with "$x<k$ ∧ $A[i]<k$ for $1<i<k$" and augment both assertions $\overline{2}$ and 3 (i.e. the conclusion of lemma 1) with "$t<k$," these additional assertions are easily verified by backward substitution using $A[i]<k$ for $1<i<k$; the latter holds everywhere in $\overline{\text{Rep}}(x)$ since $\overline{A}$ is unaltered by Rep(x).

One reason Morris said he failed using inductive assertions was that he wrote $A[A[t]]$. I avoided this by using (A1) and (A2). Going backward is not important since the proof for Rep(x) is easily done by working forward.

Lemma 2: The subroutine Enter(x,y) is defined by the following flowchart. If assertions 1a and 1b on the flowchart hold on entry, then assertions 2a - 2d hold at the exit.

Proof:

Enter (x,y) :

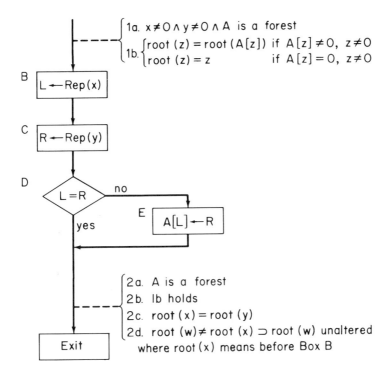

1a. $x \neq 0 \wedge y \neq 0 \wedge A$ is a forest

1b. $\begin{cases} \text{root } (z) = \text{root } (A[z]) & \text{if } A[z] \neq 0, \ z \neq 0 \\ \text{root } (z) = z & \text{if } A[z] = 0, \ z \neq 0 \end{cases}$

B $L \leftarrow \text{Rep}(x)$

C $R \leftarrow \text{Rep}(y)$

D $L = R$ no

E $A[L] \leftarrow R$

yes

2a. A is a forest
2b. 1b holds
2c. root $(x) = $ root (y)
2d. root $(w) \neq$ root $(x) \supset$ root (w) unaltered
   where root (x) means before Box B

Exit

The assertions 2a-2d are verified as follows:
First note that 1a and 1b show the assumptions for
calling Rep(x) and Rep(y) are satisfied. Hence, at
box D (using lemma 1) $L \neq 0 \wedge L=$root(x) $\wedge A[L]=0$ and
$R \neq 0 \wedge R=$root(y) $\wedge A[R]=0$.

IF $L = R$, then 2c holds. There is no change
to the forest A so 2a, 2b, and 2d hold. Assume
$L \neq R$. Then $L \neq 0$ implies A[L] is defined; after
box E, A[L]=R$\neq$0. A is still a forest since the
only change to A is at A[L], now set to R. That
is, the structure whose root is R is still a tree
since the tree whose root was L($\neq$R) is now a new

son tree of R. In symbols root (L) = root(R) =
root (A[L]) with A[L] $\neq$ 0 and L $\neq$ 0. But root (R) =
R since A[R] = 0; hence lb still holds at the exit.
Moreover, 2d holds since only root(x) is changed at
box E.

It remains to show 2c, root(x) = root(y):

root(x) = root(L)   by definition of L and
                     the change to A at box E,

        = R   by above (in showing lb
                     holds at exit),

        = root(y)   by definition of R.

To show that all array references remain in
bounds after Enter, one can augment assertion la
with "x<k $\wedge$ y<k $\wedge$ A[i]<k for 1<i<k" and assertion
2a with "A[i]<k for 1<i<k." The new 2a holds by
la and box E since R<k by the augmented assertion
3 of Rep. Finally, note that the new la is
precisely the augmentation to Rep's assertion 1,
the assumption for calling Rep.

We are now ready to prove the statement of
correctness.

Theorem 1: Let $\equiv$ denote the equivalence
relation. Let z and w be integers, 1<z,w<k. Then
each call of Enter(x,y) preserves the relation

$$z \equiv w \qquad \text{iff Equiv}(z,w).$$

(i.e. this relation could appear as both assertion
lc and assertion 2e on the flowchart for Enter(x,y).)

Proof: Since Equiv(z,w) iff Rep(z)=Rep(w) by
the definition of Equiv and since Rep(z)=root(z)
by lemma 1, the relation to prove (preserve) is

$$z \equiv w \qquad \text{iff root}(z)=\text{root}(w).$$

It is first necessary to show that lemma 2's
assumptions, la and lb, for calling Enter(x,y) are

satisfied. By assumption $x \neq 0$ and $y \neq 0$. Prior to the
first call to Enter, we have by the array initialization, $A[z]=0$, i.e. $root(z)=z$ for all z, so A is
initially a forest (of all roots). Hence, both la
and lb hold prior to the first call. For subsequent
calls to Enter, the assertions 2a and 2b guarantee
la and lb since A is changed only in Enter. (The
augmented assertion la, $x<k \wedge y \leq k \wedge A[i]<k$ for
$1<i<k$, for showing valid array references is satisfied for similar reasons: by assumption on x and
y, and first by the initialization $A[i]=0$ and
subsequently by the augmented 2a, $A[i] \leq k$ for
$1 \leq i < k$.)

The proof proceeds by cases prior to the call
of Enter(x,y) which by lemma 2, assertion 2d,
changes only $root(x)$.

1. $x \equiv y$. Thus $root(x) = root(y)$ and Enter(x,y)
   makes no change to the forest A.

2. $x \not\equiv y$. Let s be an integer, $1<s<k$, and
   consider which equivalences and roots are
   changed.

   (a) $s \equiv x$, i.e. $root(s) = root(x)$. After
   Enter(x,y) we have $root(x) = root(y)$ by 2c.
   And $root(s) = root(x)$ still holds since
   $root(s)$ was a synonym for the old $root(x)$.
   Then $s \equiv x$ and $x \equiv y$ means $x \equiv y$ iff $root(s) =$
   $root(x) = root(y)$. For this case these are
   the only changes to $z \equiv w$ iff $root(z) = root(w)$.

   (b) $s \equiv y$, i.e. $root(s) = root(y)$. After
   Enter(x,y) we have $root(x) = root(y)$. Then
   $s \equiv y$ and $x \equiv y$ means $s \equiv x$ iff $root(s) = root(y) =$
   $root(x)$.

   (c) $s \not\equiv x$, $s \not\equiv y$, i.e. $root(s) \neq root(x)$,
   $root(s) \neq root(y)$. Note that s, x, and y are
   all different else either $s \equiv x$, $s \equiv y$, or $x \equiv y$.
   After Enter(x,y) we have $root(x) = root(y)$.
   Then $s \not\equiv x \equiv y \not\equiv s$ iff $root(x) = root(y) \neq root(s)$.

Note that $z \equiv w$ iff $root(z) = root(w)$ holds prior

to the first call of Enter(x,y) since at that time
z≡w iff z=w iff root(z)=root(w) by root(z)=z   for
all z initially.

   Theorem 2:   Enter(x,y) and Equiv(x,y) each
terminate.

   Proof: Clear provided Rep(x) and Rep(y) both
terminate. This follows in one of three ways:
First, note that A is always a (finite) forest and
hence A[t]=0 eventually. Or second, note that only
roots are altered by Enter(x,y), and then only to
another root; specifically, root(x) is changed to
root(y) which, by box D of Enter(x,y), is different
from root(x) and hence no cycles in the forest are
generated. In other words, within each call to
Rep(x), the variable t does not assume the same
value twice; hence the loop in Rep(x) is executed
at most k times. Or third, employ an induction
proof based on the number of non-redundant calls to
Enter(x,y).

DISCUSSION

   It seems appropriate to comment on the discussion   in Morris (1970b). His proof and
my proof are not fundamentally different. A rough
indication of where his lemmas appear in my proof
is:

Morris	London
Lemma 1	Lemma 1
Lemma 2	Theorem 2
Lemma 3 (keystone)	Lemma 2 (keystone?)
Lemma 4	Apply lemma 1 and (A2)
	to show root(root(x))=
	root(x), i.e.
	Equiv(root(x),x)
Lemmas 5,6,7	Theorem 1

Morris calls his lemma 3 the "keystone" to his proof. Perhaps my lemma 2 is also a keystone.

My proof appears to avoid induction; however, the use of inductive assertions allows my inductions to appear only implicitly. Note, though, that there is an easy correspondence between his explicit inductions and my uses of assertions. Indeed, my proof of theorem 2 is almost explicit induction.

The notation in my assertions corresponds vaguely to his introduced functions. He notes, "Throughout [his] proof [he] was able to think of expressions ... in terms of the objects they denote rather than something to be evaluated by an interpreter." In my proof my notation similarly allowed me to think of the effect or "evaluation" or a subroutine on the data (the forest) "rather than something to be evaluated." That my proof is not as "algebraic" [his term] as his is reduces the elegance and formal checkability of my proof, but I claim it does not reduce the rigor.

I think Morris is overly pessimistic about our ability to show objects are unaltered between subroutine calls. The use of inductive assertions can do this and has. In London (1970b), the proof involves a subroutine siftup which is called in the main program. The proof for the subroutine shows that only certain parts of the array being sorted are changed. In other words, there are no side effects (beyond the statement of what siftup does). The last example in London (1970c) involves showing the absence of side effects ("nothing else is changed"). The same methods can show no change over larger units as demonstrated, for example, in London (1968). Thus, when Morris asks for "ways of combining proofs about sub-programs into proofs about larger programs without having to reprove everything," I note that this has been done in a few cases, albeit not routinely or mechanically.

Finally, I certainly agree with a point of view Morris expressed in the context of the design of programming languages. He added the emphasized words to "the traditional question, 'How easy is it to write *and prove correct* a program to do X?'"

ACKNOWLEDGEMENTS

This work is supported by the National Science Foundation under Grant GJ-583.

I thank J.H. Morris for his helpful comments.

REFERENCES

[1]   Knuth, D.E., (1968), *The Art of Computer Programming, Vol. 1 -- Fundamental Algorithms*, Addison-Wesley.

[2]   London, R.L., (1968), "Correctness of the Algol Procedure Askforhand," *Computer Sciences Technical Report No. 50*, University of Wisconsin.

[3]   ———, (1970a), "Experience with Inductive Assertions for Proving Programs Correct," *Symposium on the Semantics of Algorithmic Languages*, E. Engeler (Ed.), Springer-Verlag Lecture Notes Series, p. 236-251. Also *Computer Sciences Technical Report No. 92*, University of Wisconsin.

[4]   ———, (1970b), "Proof of Algorithms: A New Kind of Certification," *Comm. ACM*, Vol. 13, June, 1970, p. 371-373.

[5]   ———, (1970c), "Proving Programs Correct: Some Techniques and Examples," *BIT*, Vol. 10, No. 2, p. 168-182.

[6]   Morris, J.H. (1970a), "Another Recursion Induction Principle," *Comm. ACM*, Vol. 14, May 1971, 351-354.

[7]   ———,(1970b), "A Correctness Proof Using
Recursively Defined Functions."   This
proceedings.

FORMAL SEMANTIC DEFINITION AND THE PROOF OF COMPILER CORRECTNESS

John McCarthy
Stanford University

The talk by Professor McCarthy was essentially a tutorial based on earlier work which may be found in the references cited below.

[1]   McCarthy, J., "Computer Programs for Checking Mathematical Proofs, *Proc. Sympos. Pure Math. Vol. 5*, Amer. Math. Soc., 1962, pp. 219-227.

[2]   ——, "A Basis for a Mathematical Theory of Computation," *Computer Programming and Formal Systems*, Ed. by P. Braffort and D. Hershberg, North Holland, 1963.

[3]   ——, "Towards a Mathematical Theory of Computation," *Proc. Internat. Congr. on Information Processing*, 1962

[4]   ——, "A Formal Description of a Subset of Algol," *Proc. Conf. on Formal Language Description Languages*, Vienna, 1964.

[5]   ——, and Painter, J., "Correctness of a Compiler for Arithmetic Expressions," *Proc. Symp. Appl. Math.*, AMS, Vol. 19, 1967.

AN INDUCTIVE PROOF TECHNIQUE FOR INTERPRETER EQUIVALENCE

Clement L. McGowan
Center for Computer and Information Sciences
Brown University

A general inductive proof technique is presented here which has been successfully used in establishing the correctness and equivalence of interpreters for the lambda calculus and for block structured languages.

The semantics of programming languages is sometimes formally defined by an abstract interpreter (see, e.g., [3]). In such a case the interpreter definition should stress clarity and conciseness rather than being a guide to an efficient implementation of the defined language. Accordingly an actual implementation will usually differ markedly from the formal semantic specification. The question then arises: is the actual implementation correct? That is, for every program P in the defined language, does the actual implementation representing the computation of P yield the same result as the formal interpreter applied to P? When this question is formalized we see that the actual implementation is itself an interpreter and its correctness is a special case of interpreter equivalence. In this context the observation of Wegner [8] is of interest:

...the hard problem in compiler correctness proofs is proving the equivalence of
source and target language interpreters,
and progress in proving compilers correct
is directly dependent on progress in
proofs of correctness and equivalence of
interpreters.

This paper presents an inductive proof technique for
interpreter equivalence which has been used successfully in several settings.

To fix notation and terminology we say a *snapshot* (instantaneous description of an information
structure) consists of a finite number of immediate
components, each selected by a distinct simple
selector such that each component is either a snapshot or an atom (elementary object). That is, a
snapshot is a composite object in the sense of [3]
where the sets of simple selectors and elementary
objects are countable and depend upon the set of
snapshots which are defined (by an abstract syntax).
The reader unfamiliar with the Vienna Definition
Language can exercise his intuition because snapshots
are just the set of information structures which may
occur during a computation and include cells, stacks,
lists, trees, counters, pointers, etc.

An *interpreter* or *information structure model*
$M = (I, I_0, F)$ is a triple where I is a countable set
of snapshots, $I_0 \subseteq I$ is the set of initial snapshots
and F is a finite set of functions, $f: I \to I \cup \{\phi\}$
(see [8,10]).

A *computation* by the interpreter $M = (I, I_0, F)$
is a sequence of snapshots

$$S_0, S_1, \ldots, S_{j-1}, S_j, \ldots$$

each an element of I such that $S_0 \varepsilon I_0$ and for each S_j
in the computation (with $j > 0$) there is some $f \varepsilon F$
such that $f(S_{j-1}) = S_j$. If there exists a snapshot
S_n in the computation such that $f(S_n) = \phi$ for each
f in F, then the computation on S_0 is said to *halt*
at the *final snapshot* S_n.

Intuitively an interpreter M = (I, I_0, F) for a programming language L consists of a specification of the initial representations I_0 of programs in L (the abstract syntax for L), the set of information structures I which can arise during computations by M (the set of states of M) and the instructions F which constitute the interpreter proper (the semantic function). Typically the application of a function (instruction) from $F = \{f_1, \ldots, f_k\}$ to a snapshot S is determined by a conditional statement:

if P_1 *then* f_1 *else if* P_2 *then* f_2 ...

else if P_k *then* f_k

with the usual meaning — first test whether the predicate P_1 is true of snapshot S; if it is apply f_1 to S; else test whether P_2 is true of S ... and so on. An interpreter restrained by such a conditional statement is said to be *deterministic*.

Note that in the definition of an interpreter we did not have

f:I → {finite subset of I U {φ}}

That is, our interpreter is sequential. For the additional considerations which associative or non-deterministic interpreters introduce into interpreter equivalence proofs see [7]. We restrict our attention to deterministic interpreters.

If M = (I, I_0, F) is a deterministic interpreter and $S_0 \varepsilon I_0$, then there is a unique computation of M which corresponds to S_0:

$$S_0, S_1, \ldots, S_{j-1}, S_j, \ldots$$

and so at most one final snapshot S_n corresponds to S_0 for the interpreter M. We introduce a predicate *is-final* and a selector OUTPUT for the set I of snapshots. If $S \varepsilon I$, then is-final(S) is true if and only if S is a final snapshot — i.e., if f(S) = φ for all fεF. If is-final(S), then OUTPUT(S) is the output component of the final snapshot S. We can now regard an interpreter M as a partial function defined on I_0 as follows:

$$M(S_0) = \begin{cases} \text{OUTPUT}(S_n) \; \textit{WHERE} \text{ is-final}(S_n) \text{ and} \\ S_0,S_1,\ldots,S_{n-1},S_n \text{ is the com-} \\ \text{putation of M for } S_0 \varepsilon I_0. \\[1em] \text{undefined otherwise} \end{cases}$$

Two interpreters $M = (I,I_0,F)$ and $M' = (I',I_0,F')$
are equivalent if the corresponding partial functions
M and M' are equivalent. That is, M and M' are
equivalent if

$(\forall S_0 \varepsilon I_0)$ [the M computation on S_0 halts $\Leftrightarrow$ the M'
          computation on S_0 halts

                    and

          if the M computation halts, then
          $M(S_0) \equiv M'(S_0)$]

where "$\equiv$" denotes equivalence of outputs and whose
precise definition is dependent on the set of
possible OUTPUT components for snapshots of M and
M' (a special case of "$\equiv$" would be equality). Note
that M and M' have the same set I_0 of initial snapshots. This simply requires that interpreters are
equivalent with respect to some lanaugage whose
programs are represented by I_0. This is not overly
restrictive since the first part of an interpreter
computation could be effectively a pre-pass which
transforms an initial snapshot $S_0 \varepsilon I_0$ into some other
representation.

     Thus formulated, the general problem of whether
two interpreters are equivalent is recursively
unsolvable, since the interpreters could be Turing
machines. However, the most frequently occurring
situation where the question of interpreter equivalence is posed is where interpreter M is given and
interpreter M' is constructed to be (by intention)
equivalent to M. For example, M might be a formal
interpreter which defines the semantics of a programming language and M' the formalization of the

actual implementation of that language, or M' might
be proposed as a more efficient (by some measure)
evaluation strategy for an algorithm than the
original strategy expressed formally by M. This is
to say that in practice the problem of interpreter
equivalence can sometimes be quite tractable, despite
the unsolvability of the general problem, since the
two given interpreters are, by intention at least,
equivalent rather than being two arbitrary information structure models. The proof technique which
we now present is based upon the observation,
confirmed by experience, that if M' is constructed
with the intention that it be equivalent to M, then
for a given input $S_0 \varepsilon I_0$ it is likely that some of
the intermediate snapshots in the M computation of
S_0 are related to some of the intermediate snapshots
in the M' computation of S_0. Thus "the trick" is
to construct mappings of the two computations which
formally express these intermediate relationships.

Given interpreters $M = (I, I_0, F)$ and $M' = (I', I_0, F')$, to show M is equivalent to M' construct
two functions $\phi: I \to X$ and $\phi': I' \to X$ having a common
range set X with an equality relationship "="
defined for members of X such that for all $S_0 \varepsilon I_0$ if

$$S_0, S_1, \ldots, S_j, \ldots \quad \text{is the M computation of } S_0$$

and

$$S_0, S'_1, \ldots, S'_k, \ldots \quad \text{is the M' computation of } S_0$$

then we have:

(1) $\phi(S_0) = \phi'(S_0)$

(2) If $\phi(S_j) = \phi'(S'_k)$
    and (a) *not* is-final(S_j) *and not* is-final(S'_k),
        then $(\exists\ p \geq 1, q \geq 1)[\phi(S_{j+p}) = \phi'(S'_{k+q})]$
    and (b) is-final(S'_k), then
        $(\exists\ n \geq 0)[\text{is-final}(S_{j+n})$
        and OUTPUT$(S_{j+n}) \equiv$ OUTPUT$(S'_k)]$

and (c) is-final(S_j), then

$(\exists\ n\geq 0)$ [is-final(S'_{k+n})

and OUTPUT(S_j) $\equiv$ OUTPUT(S'_{k+n})]

Clauses (2b) and (2c) suffice for establishing the desired equivalence result and clauses (1) and (2a) are the inductive formulation. Intuitively (1) states that the two computations begin equivalently, (2a) says that if the computations have progressed equivalently up to intermediate snapshots S_j and S'_k, then there are subsequent snapshots S_{j+p} and S'_{k+q} where the computations are again equivalent, and (2b, 2c) assert that the corresponding M and M' computations terminate equivalently (if they terminate at all).

M computation of S_0

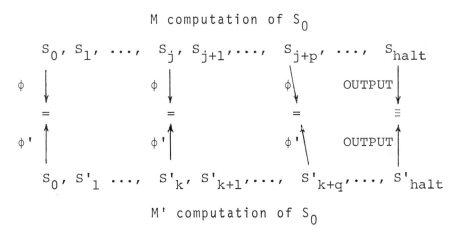

M' computation of S_0

It is of interest to note that several inductive proof techniques are specializations of the above. For example, the author has proved the correctness of three distinct lambda calculus interpreters where:

M = (I,I_0,F) is the mathematical formulation of the lambda calculus.

I_0 = I = {well-formed expressions of the lambda calculus} and

F = {Renaming Rule, Reduction Rule}

and M is made deterministic by always performing the leftmost (or rightmost) possible reduction for a given expression. Correctness of a lambda calculus interpreter M' is just the equivalence of M' with M. In the course of establishing these correctness results it was found that Landin's SECD machine [2] does not completely evaluate all expressions of the lambda calculus. However, a straightforward modification produced a modified SECD machine $M'_\lambda = (I'_\lambda , I_0, F'_\lambda)$ where snapshots in I'_λ had six immediate components: stack, environment, control, dump, output, and a unique name counter; and F'_λ was an extension of Landin's TRANSFORM function. This modified SECD machine M'_λ was proved equivalent to the formal definition M of the lambda calculus, and hence correct, using a specialization of the above proof technique where: $X=I=I_0=\{$expressions of the lambda calculus$\}$, ϕ = identity function, for $S\epsilon I$ OUTPUT(S) = S, and "output equivalence" and "equality in X" were both "equivalent up to renaming" [see 4, 5]. Of special interest is the fact that the ϕ' mapping function from states of M'_λ to expressions in a reduction sequence was obtained constructively by restricting the TRANSFORM function of F'_λ. A similar approach established the correctness of Wegner's Basic Lambda Calculus Machine defined in [9] and a lambda calculus interpreter satisfying the fixed program restriction [see 5, 6]. The particular specialization of the proof technique to $X = I = I_0, \phi$ = identity function and p = 1 in (2a) with ϕ' being constructed by a restriction of F' appears to have wide applicability and is used in [7] to show the equivalence of infix and postfix evaluation of arithmetic expressions. Step-by-step interpreter equivalence is given by taking p = q = 1 and n = 0 in clause (2).

Berry [1] has used a variant of the above mapping technique to establish the formal equivalence of the copy rule for block structured languages with the contour model implementation of such languages. A corollary to this result is that the copy rule implies a retention strategy (i.e., deallocation *only* when no longer accessible) rather than a deletion strategy (i.e., deallocation upon block exit) for block structured languages. In the case of ALGOL 60 these two evaluation strategies can be shown to be equivalent. However, when programming languages have such features as pointers, procedure and label variables they are no longer equivalent.

Regarding the lambda calculus as a relatively simple but non-trivial block structured programming language we can say that the mapping proof technique presented here has been successfully used in investigating the correctness and equivalence of interpreters for block structured programming languages.

REFERENCES

[1]   Berry, D., "Block Structure: Retention or Deletion?", *Third ACM Symposium on Theory of Computing*, 1971.

[2]   Landin, P., "The Mechanical Evaluation of Expressions," *Computer Journal* 6, 4, 1964.

[3]   Lucas, P., and Walk, K., "On the Formal Description of Pl/I," *Annual Review in Automatic Programming* 6, 3, 1969.

[4]   McGowan, C., "The Correctness of a Modified SECD Machine," *Second ACM Symposium on Theory of Computing*, 1970.

[5]   ——————— , "Correctness Results for Lambda Calculus Interpreters, *Ph.D. Thesis*, Cornell University, 1971.

[6]   ——————— , "On the Equivalence of Mechanical Evaluation Strategies," *ACM Symposium on Programming Language Definition*, 1969.

[7]   ——————— , and Wegner, P., "The Equivalence of Sequential and Associative Information

structure Models", *ACM Symposium on Data Structures in Programming Languages*, 1971.

[8]   Wegner, P., "Programming Language Semantics," *this volume*.

[9]   ————— , *Programming Languages, Information Structures and Machine Organization*, McGraw-Hill, 1968.

[10]   ————— , "Three Computer Cultures — Computer Technology, Computer Mathematics and Computer Science," *Advances in Computers* 10, 1970.

ACKNOWLEDGEMENT

This work was supported in part by the National Science Foundation under Grant GJ-28074.

PROGRAMMING LANGUAGE SEMANTICS

Peter Wegner
Brown University

(Editor's Note: This is a considerably expanded version of the talk given at the symposium.)

This paper contrasts and compares a number of approaches to programming-language semantics, placing special emphasis on the operational approach in which the "meaning" of program constituents is defined in terms of their operational effect during program execution. Both descriptive and formal characteristics of operational semantic models are considered. Problems relating to interpreter definition and to proving assertions about interpreters are used as canonical examples to illustrate that operational semantic models are appropriate in the descriptive and formal study of complex classes of computations with undecidable termination problems.

A copy rule model of block structure languages with procedure variables, label variables and parameters called by value, reference and name, is developed in some detail. A number of models of implementation which are "equivalent" but "more efficient" than the copy rule model are introduced in order to motivate the notion of interpreter equivalence.

A number of alternative notions of computational equivalence are contrasted and compared. The weakest of these, referred to as output equivalence, is defined in terms of homomorphic mappings of domains and ranges which preserve "computational equivalence" between inputs and outputs. Restrictions on mappings of domains and ranges are considered, and the application to proofs of compiler correctness is discussed. Stronger definitions of computational equivalence are introduced which constrain the sequence in which corresponding instructions of corresponding computations are executed, and provide an appropriate framework for proofs of equivalence of interpreters. Two proof techniques for equivalence of interpreters known as the Lucas twin machine technique and the McGowan mapping technique are considered in some detail.

The twin machine and mapping techniques are compared with techniques developed for other models for proving assertions about programs such as McCarthy's recursion equation model and the annotated flowchart model introduced by Floyd and elaborated by Manna, Hoare and others. It is shown that the McCarthy and Painter proof of compiler correctness does not generalize because it does not adequately distinguish between static program structure and the dynamic structure of the record of execution. The Floyd technique cannot easily be adapted to proofs of equivalence of very complex but very similar programs, since an equivalence proof using annotated flowcharts as a normal form for programs depends on the complexity of the objects being proved equivalent rather than on the complexity of the mapping function between objects being proved equivalent.

It is proposed that the semantics of programming languages be defined in terms of semi-constructive equivalence classes of interpreters, where the criterion of equivalence is defined in terms of provability by a specific class of proof techniques.

TABLE OF CONTENTS

1. What is Semantics?
2. Information Structure Models
3. Descriptive and Formal Accomplishments of
      Operational Modelling
4. The Equivalence of Interpreters
5. A Copy Rule Model for Identifier Accessing
6. Implementation of the Copy Rule Model
7. Twin Machine Proofs of Interpreter
      Equivalence
8. Output-Equivalent Interpreters
9. Infix and Postfix Expression Evaluation
10. The McGowan Mapping Technique
11. McCarthy's Model of Semantics
12. Floyd's Model of Semantics
13. The Predicate Calculus with Assignment,
      Equality and Control
14. Some Observations on Semantic Modelling
15. Language Definition by Semi-Constructive
      Interpreter Equivalence Classes

Acknowledgements

Bibliography

1. WHAT IS SEMANTICS?

Semantics may be defined as the study of the relation between objects and their representations. Usually we are given a set of representations of objects, specified in a "language" which allows relations between objects to be expressed, and wish to say something about the "meaning" or "denotation" of the representations.

Thus *natural language semantics* may be defined
as the study of the relation between written or ver-
bal symbols (character strings or phonemes) and the
objects which they denote. *Programming language
semantics* may be defined as the study of the relation between programs (symbol strings) and objects
denoted by programs. *Mathematical semantics* may be
defined as the study of the relation between mathematical expressions and the objects which they denote.

The notion of semantics adopted by mathematical
logicians [T1,M11] is very much in the spirit of the
above definition. Logicians deal with *languages*
whose *expressions* consist of *symbols* whose *meaning*
is restricted to a specific universe of discourse.
The symbols are grouped into classes and the
"meaning" of symbols in each class is allowed to
vary over a carefully controlled domain of interpretation. For example, the domain of interpretation of symbols of the first-order predicate
calculus may be characterized as follows:

a) *Logical operator symbols* such as quantifiers ($\forall$, $\exists$) and propositional connectives
($\land,\lor,\lnot,\supset$) which have a *fixed interpretation* defined
by logical axioms.

b) *Constant symbols* which, in an interpreted
system, denote specific elements of a domain D and
in an uninterpreted system denote unspecified
elements of an unspecified domain D.

c) *Variable symbols* which are interpreted as
mathematical variables over the domain D of constants.

d) *n-ary function symbols* whose interpretation
may vary over the space of n-ary functions from
D^n into D.

e) *Logical constant symbols* which represent
the values *true* and *false* and have a fixed meaning
in all interpretations, just as quantifiers and
logical connectives.

f) *n-ary predicate symbols* whose interpretations may vary over the space of n-ary predicates
from D^n into the values *true* and *false*.

The predicate calculus may be rigorously defined
by specifying the class of all valid expressions in
a *syntactic notation*, by specifying for each symbol
permitted by the syntax the *domain of denotations*
over which it may vary, and by recursively specifying the *semantics* of syntactically valid expressions
in terms of the semantics of component subexpressions. Certain commonly occurring mathematical
systems may be conveniently defined by introducing
specific symbols with specific interpretations into
the general model of the predicate calculus. For
example, the predicate calculus with equality is
obtained from the general predicate calculus by
introducing a binary predicate symbol "=" whose
meaning is defined in terms of "axioms for equality."
Groups, rings and other algebraic structures may
similarly be defined by introducing specific constant
symbols and function symbols with axiomatically-
defined meanings into the predicate calculus.

The predicate calculus allows a wide variety
of specific mathematical systems to be defined by
restricting the interpretation of constant symbols,
function symbols and predicate symbols to specific
elements or classes of elements in their domain.
However, there is no provision in the predicate
calculus for varying the mechanism of function
composition (function application). Function composition is always specified by the literal juxtaposition of the function to be applied and the
arguments to which the function is to be applied.

The advent of digital computers has resulted
in notations for function specification with more
flexible mechanisms for specifying the sequence in
which functions are to be applied to their arguments.
In particular, the *assignment operator* allows
function values to be stored for use in subsequent
function evaluation, and *conditional branching
operations* allow direct control over the sequence
in which functions are to be applied to their

arguments. Notations which require function application to be specified by the literal juxtaposition
of a function and its arguments will be called
algebraic notations, while notations which allow
the assignment of values to computational variables
and conditional branching will be called *computational notations*.

A number of semantic models of computational
notations have been developed, including those of
Ianov [I1,R2], Paterson [P1], Luckham, Park and
Paterson [L7], Floyd [F2] and Manna [M1]. Each of
these models superimposes the computational notions
of assignment and instruction sequencing on an
algebraic notation for expression evaluation.
Semantic models which superimpose assignment and
instruction sequencing on an algebraic notation are
referred to as *program schemes*. Program schemes
allow the meaning of algebraic symbols to vary over
the same domain as the predicate calculus, and
associate a fixed interpretation with assignment
and instruction sequencing which allows forms of
function composition which result from the execution
of instructions on a digital computer to be directly
modelled.

The semantics of program schemes, just as that
of the predicate calculus, may be defined in terms
of the denotations of symbols that occur in program
schemes. Constant symbols, function symbols and
predicate symbols of program schemes may vary over
the same domain of denotations as in algebraic
notations. Variable symbols denote cells whose
values may be updated by assignment operators as
opposed to mathematical variables over the domain
D. The semantics of assignment and instruction
sequencing is generally defined by defining the
sequences of states which result during instruction
execution for specific interpretations of constant
symbols, function symbols and predicate symbols.

In developing a semantic model for a class of
objects such as the class of computable functions,
three levels of thinking may be distinguished:

a)   The class of objects being modelled

b)   The computational formalism used to
     model the class of objects

c)   The semantic model used to define the
     semantics of the computational formalism.

The class of computable functions has proved to
be very robust with respect to different formalisms
for its definitions. It has been modelled by set-
theoretical models based on the predicate calculus,
generatively modelled by phrase-structure grammars,
defined by a recognition criterion in terms of
Turing machines or other classes of automata
(acceptors), functionally defined by the lambda
calculus, and computationally defined by any sufficiently powerful digital computer or programming
language.

Different computational formalisms lead to
different styles of computation of specific
functions. In computer science we are on the whole
interested in formalisms which closely model the
style of computation of actual digital computers.
Thus the formalism of program schemes is of greater
interest than the formalism of basic set theory or
of the lambda calculus.

Once the computational formalism has been
chosen, there are still a large number of alter-
natives in fixing the model for expressing the
semantics of the computational formalism. Three
classes of semantic models, respectively referred
to as abstract models, input-output models and
operational models, will be distinguished.

a)   In *abstract semantic models* the objects
being represented are assumed to have an existence
independently of any representation, and it is the
purpose of the semantic definition to characterize
the "essence" of such independently-existing
objects in a representation-independent way. This
approach leads to attempts to reduce computational
notations to mathematical notations, since mathe-

matical models are assumed to capture the representation-independent essence of computational
phenomena. For example, Landin's model of programming languages in terms of the lambda calculus [L2]
and Scott's model of computable functions in terms
of a class of mathematical lattices [S2] are abstract
semantic models.

b)   In *input-output models* of semantics the
functions we wish to compute are characterized in
terms of the relation between inputs and outputs
which they determine. This approach to the assigning of meanings to programs was considered by
Floyd [F2] and developed by Manna [M1], Hoare [H3]
and Manna and Waldinger [M2]. Meaning is defined
in terms of a correctness criterion which constitutes
a necessary and sufficient condition for a program
to realize a given function.

Semantic definition by a relation between
inputs and outputs has led to proofs that programs
correctly implement the semantic definition [F2],
and even to techniques for synthesizing programs
for their input-output specification [M2]. However,
this form of semantic definition is not appropriate
as a universal normal form for specifying the
semantics of programming languages for the following
reasons:

1.   Although many of the computations that
we wish to specify in practice are conveniently
specified by a relation between inputs and outputs,
there are some computations which cannot be specified in this way. For example, programming languages generally have an undecidable halting problem. We cannot use input-output semantics to
uniformly specify the semantics of an interpreter
for a programming language in terms of a relation
between inputs and outputs. Programming language
semantics must therefore be expressed in terms of
a different kind of semantic model.

2.   Input-output semantics regards all programs
which realize the same function as equivalent.

However, computer scientists are often interested
in differences between programs which realize the
same function. The language designer is interested
in differences of *representation* of programs in
different programming languages. The language
implementer is interested in differences of *implementation* of a given program in a given programming
language.

c) In *operational models of semantics* we are
concerned not only with the relation between inputs
and outputs, but also with the *path* by which we get
from the input to the output and with the *information structures* which are generated along this path.
The path is defined by the sequence of executed
instructions and is sometimes referred to as the
execution sequence, while the sequence of information structures (snapshots, states) generated along
this path is referred to as the *computation
sequence*.

Operational models distinguish between different ways of computing the same function, and allow
computations to be grouped into finer equivalence
classes than input-output models. Moreover, when
semantics is defined in terms of execution sequences
and computation sequences, correctness and equivalence of classes of computations may be defined by
induction on elements of the sequence rather than
in terms of a relation between inputs and outputs.
Operational notions of correctness and equivalence
may be defined for non-terminating computations
with infinite execution and computational sequences
by induction on elements of the sequence, while
input-ouput notions of correctness and equivalence
cannot easily be extended to non-terminating
computations. Thus operational semantics allows
the notions of correctness and equivalence of computations to be defined for a larger domain than
input-output semantics and allows a greater range
of computational phenomena to be modelled by allowing different ways of computing the same function
to be modelled by different equivalence classes.

Examples:

a)   The class of integers may be thought of as objects which exist independently of any specific representation and independently of specific operators such as addition or multiplication which may be applicable to them. This point of view is sometimes referred to as a Platonic point of view, since Plato [P2] assumed that objects have an existence independently of any specific representation.

b)   The class of integers may be defined in a representation-independent way by a set of axioms which constitute a necessary and sufficient set of behaviors for a representation to be considered a representation of the integers. Peano's axioms [M11] are an example of a representation-independent set of axioms which is intended to characterize the integers.

c)   The class of integers may be characterized by a specific programming language for representing integers and operations on integers.

The semantics of a specific programming language may be characterized in a variety of different ways either in terms of input-output semantics or in terms of operational semantics which defines the semantics of symbols in terms of the transformational effect to which they give rise in a specific implementation. There is generally a variety of different implementation-dependent operational definitions of semantics associated with a given definition of input-output semantics.

Operational models define semantics in terms of *observable* state transformations which occur during computations, and may be compared to operational models in other disciplines. The operational approach became fashionable in physics with the development of relativity theory and quantum mechanics and led to behaviorism in psychology and intuitionism in mathematics. In computer science, just as in other disciplines, the operational point

of view assumes that the existence of independent
objects denoted by representations is irrelevant
to the semantic model, and that the meaning of a
class of representations is completely determined
by observable transformations to which the representations give rise.

A class of objects A has no absolute operational
meaning but only a relative meaning relative to a
frame of reference B which constitutes the defining
semantic model. A semantic model defines a binary
relation R(A,B) between the class A of objects
being defined and the defining frame of reference
B. A given class A of objects has different meanings
relative to different defining models. From this
point of view it is natural that the mathematician
may associate a different semantic model with the
class of computable functions than the computer
scientist. The computer scientist should choose a
class of semantic models which emphasizes computational attributes of the computable functions while
the mathematician should choose a class of models
which emphasizes mathematical attributes.

The mathematician regards questions of representation and implementation of functions as
tactical questions which have little strategic
importance, while the computer scientist regards
the study of relations among representations and
implementations as central to computer science. It
is therefore appropriate that the semantic models
of computer science should be sensitive to differences in representation of computable functions and
to differences in implementation of a given function
representation.

2. INFORMATION STRUCTURE MODELS

The operational approach leads to the definition of programming languages in terms of observable
sequences of information structure transformations
generated by programs during execution. A general
class of models for the operational specification

of programming languages in terms of execution-time
information structure transformations [W4,W5,W6]
may be defined as follows:

Definition: An *information structure model* is a
triple $M = (I,I^0,F)$ where I is a countable set of
information structures (structured states), $I^0 \subseteq I$
is a set of initial representations, and F is a
finitely representable set of unary operations
(primitive instructions) whose domain and range is
a subset of I.

We shall be concerned principally with the
following special case of information structure
models:

Definition: A *deterministic* (sequential) information structure model is one which for all $I_j \varepsilon I$ has
at most one element $f \varepsilon F$ applicable to I_j. Since
all information structures considered here are
deterministic we shall use the term "information
structure model" to mean "deterministic information
structure model."

Definition: A *computation* in a (deterministic)
information structure model $M = (I,I^0,F)$ is a
sequence $I_0,I_1,\ldots$ of elements of I such that
$I_0 \varepsilon I^0$ and for $j=0,1,2,\ldots,$ $I_{j+1} = f(I_j)$ for some
$f \varepsilon F$.

Definition: A *terminating computation* is a computation which, for some integer n, generates an I_n
to which no element $f \varepsilon F$ is applicable.

Information structure models define the
semantics of programs and programming languages
operationally in terms of a specific *implementation*
or *interpreter*.

Example: An implementation of a programming language such as ALGOL 60 may be defined by a set of
initial representations I^0 of programs with their
data, a set of information configurations I which
may occur during the execution of programs in the

given representation, and a set of primitive operators F which specify how configurations I are
transformed both for the execution of explicit
operators such as "+" and for the execution of
implicit operators such as entry to and exit from
blocks and procedures. In the case of ALGOL 60
the set I of states which may occur during
execution is richer than the set I^0 of initial
representations, since all elements of I^0 have an
empty stack component while elements of I may have
a non-empty stack component.

Syntactic definition mechanisms such as the
BNF notation used in the specification of ALGOL 60
[N2] were designed for the specification of only
the set I^0 of initial representations of computations. Semantic definition mechanisms such as the
Vienna definition language [L6] syntactically
specify both the set I^0 of initial representation
and the set I of computational states, and semantically specify the state transitions F in terms of
conditional expressions of the form

$$[p_1 \rightarrow a_1; \; p_2 \rightarrow a_2; \ldots; \; p_n \rightarrow a_n;]$$

where for i = 1,2,...,n p_i specifies a predicate
to be satisfied by the current state and a_i specifies
a state transformation to be performed if p_i is the
first true predicate of the conditional expression.

A complete programming language definition
requires the sets I^0, I of information configurations
to be specified in a *syntactic metalanguage* and the
set F of primitive instructions to be specified in
a *semantic metalanguage*. Such a definition may, in
the case of a complex language such as PL/I, take
many hundreds of pages [W2]. However, there are
many attributes of implementations which can be
characterized in terms of gross attributes of
structural components of I^0 and I. For example, it
is generally possible to characterize information
structures I by triples (C,P,D) where C is a control
component, P is a program component and D is a data

component, and to classify implementations in terms
of gross attributes of C, P and D, such as invariance
in the case of reentrant (fixed) program components
P, and stack structure in the case of data components
D.

The concept of an information structure model
provides a framework for the *controlled variation*
of the level of detail of semantic models of programming languages, allowing us to emphasize precisely those attributes which we wish to study on
any particular occasion.

Programming languages may be syntactically
characterized by notations for the specification
of *sets* which constitute valid programs of the programming language and semantically characterized
by notations for the specification of *sequences*
which constitute valid computations of the programming language. Sets are a *static* concept appropriate
to the study of program representations, while
sequences are a *dynamic* concept appropriate to the
study of program execution. The present view of the
relation between syntax and semantics is analogous
to the distinction in physics between statics and
dynamics. However, physicists are constrained to
study laws of motion determined by nature while
computer scientists are free to define arbitrary
state transition functions and to study the
"discrete" laws of transformation determined by
specific state transition functions or classes of
state transition functions. The tools for the study
of continuous state transition functions in analogue
and process control computers are in fact quite
similar to the tools used by the physicist. Although
the mathematics required for the study of "discrete
transformational systems" is not as well understood
as that required for the study of the dynamics of
physical systems, it is likely that within fifty
years or so such mathematics will occupy as central
a position in applied mathematics as the theory of
differential equations does today. Moreover, the
set-theoretic framework currently used to characterize mathematical semantics may well have the same
relation to computational semantic concepts as the

techniques of statics have to the techniques of dynamics.

3. DESCRIPTIVE AND FORMAL ACCOMPLISHMENTS OF OPERATIONAL MODELLING

The value of a class of models in computer science must be justified by the insights and understanding it provides of the phenomena of computer science. We shall briefly outline some of the accomplishments of the operational view of semantics advocated above, and then consider in detail the structure of operational proofs of interpreter equivalence.

Operational models of semantics which define programming languages in terms of the information structures which they generate during execution are useful both at the descriptive and at the formal level. The following is a partial enumeration of descriptive operational models which have helped us to gain insight and understanding into the structure of programming languages.

a) Descriptive Models

The LISP APPLY function was probably the first systematic attempt to define a programming language in terms of its implementation [M6]. This model, which was developed as early as 1960, has had an enormous influence on the subsequent modelling of programming languages, and has strongly influenced the work of Landin [L1], Lucas and Walk [L6] and many others.

The work on register transfer languages and the definition of the IBM 360 system in APL [F1] may be regarded as the application of the operational approach to the definition of computers.

The definition of PL/I [W2], ALGOL 60 [N2] and other languages in the Vienna definition language [L6] constitutes a practical demonstration that

even very complex languages may be defined operationally in terms of their implementation and has
provided practical experience which will be inval-
uable to the development of fugure operational
definitions of programming languages. This work
represents a great step forward in our understanding
of how programming languages should be defined.

A number of recent papers in the Proceedings
of the Symposium on Data Structures in Programming
Languages [B1,J1,M10,O1,W1,W6] constitute a
coordinated effort to develop operational semantic
models of programming languages and digital
computers. These papers include a paper on the
contour model for block structure processes which
allows execution-time configurations arising during
the execution of block structure languages to be
modelled two-dimensionally [J1], a model of the
B6700 computer in terms of execution-time information structure transformations [O1], an operational model of storage structures in higher level languages [W1], an operational definition of the language "Oregano" using the contour model as a metalanguage [B1], and a paper on operational techniques for proving the equivalence of interpreters
[M10].

b)   Formal Models

McCarthy proposed an operational approach to
proving assertions about programs as early as 1962
[M3]. The proof techniques advocated by McCarthy
are illustrated in the McCarthy and Painter proof
of a correctness of a compiler for a simple class
of arithmetic expressions [M5]. The reasons why
their proof technique did not generalize to more
complex proofs of interpreter correctness are
discussed in a later section of this paper.

Floyd's approach of assigning meanings to
programs [F2] may be described as a semi-operational
approach since it associates meanings with programs
rather than program implementations. The relation
between Floyd's approach and the full operational
approach advocated here is discussed in later

sections.

The formalism of the Vienna definition language has given rise to an interesting class of
proofs of interpreter equivalence [L4,H2,J2] which
prove the equivalence of a number of different
techniques of identifier accessing in block structure languages.

McGowan [M7,M8,M10] has developed a number of
proofs of equivalence of lambda calculus interpreters.

Berry [B2] has developed a proof of equivalence
of the contour model and the literal substitution
model of block structure semantics.

The structure of interpreter equivalence
proofs of the Vienna definition group and of
McGowan and Berry is discussed in greater detail
below. It is shown that each proof technique
determines equivalence classes of interpreters
which are provably equivalent under that proof
technique, and it is suggested that definition of
a programming language in terms of such a provably
equivalent class of interpreters may often be more
meaningful than a more abstract definition of a
programming language in terms of a set of axioms
which constitute a necessary and sufficient set of
behaviors for an object to be considered an instance
of the programming language.

Before considering the general question of
equivalence classes of interpreters we shall
exhibit a number of specific instances of equivalent interpreters and introduce a specific proof
technique which imposes a specific equivalence
relation on interpreters.

4. THE EQUIVALENCE OF INTERPRETERS

A given programming language may be realized by a large number of different interpreters. The choice of a specific interpreter as the programming language definition is dictated in part by the purposes for which the programming language definition is to be used. For example, a definition which aims at *conceptual clarity* may use a set of primitives that is conceptually simple but impractical on existing computers, while a definition which aims at *execution-time efficiency* may use a conceptually more complex implementation technique that involves tricks and shortcuts which improve efficiency but may be justified only by subtle reasoning.

The tradeoffs between conceptual clarity* and computer-oriented practicability may be illustrated at the simplest level by comparing infix and postfix evaluation for simple classes of arithmetic expressions. A direct infix interpreter for arithmetic expressions such as ((3*4)+(5*6)) would specify that any subexpressions of the form (i*j) or (i+j), where i and j are integers, may be asynchronously transformed into its value (see section 9). A postfix interpreter for the corresponding expression 34*56*+ would specify the left-to-right execution of successive symbols of the program string using a data stack for storing intermediate values. The infix interpreter has a certain mathematical simplicity but the associative recognition of subexpressions of the form (i+j) or (i*j) and the replacement of subexpressions by their values would require computers with associative memories and

---

*The notion "conceptual clarity" is clearly a subjective rather than an objective notion, since it depends on the concepts with which one is initially familiar. In the present context the notion of literal substitution of a variable-length substring in the body of a second string, which is a computationally complex notion, is assumed to be a conceptually primitive notion.

distributed processing intelligence and is therefore impractical on existing computers. Postfix evaluation requires a slightly more complex statement of the transformation rule (see section 9) but can be directly implemented on existing computers.

The interpreters for infix and postfix evaluation have their counterparts in interpreters for nested function evaluation. Evaluation of nested functions such as f(g(x),h(x)) is mathematically specified by a non-deterministic interpreter which evaluates g(x) and h(x) asynchronously. Nested functions are more easily evaluated on existing computers by converting the initial representation into the postfix form x g x h f and using a data stack for evaluation.

The lambda calculus is essentially a precise notation for function specification. The evaluation of lambda expressions may be defined mathematically in terms of asynchronous non-deterministic renaming and reduction rules, and may be defined computationally by a number of alternative sequential interpreters [W3].

In the case of arithmetic expressions, nested functions and the lambda calculus, evaluation rules defined by mathematicians before computers became available have turned out to be unsuitable for the direct definition of computer evaluation. However, sequential interpreters for nested functions and the lambda calculus have been proved equivalent to interpreters which directly implement the mathematical evaluation rules [M7]. The structure of these proofs is further discussed in section 10.

Block structure languages have a nested function structure with "local" bound variables that is analogous to the lambda calculus. The semantics of block entry and procedure call was defined in the ALGOL 60 report in terms of substitution rules and copy rules which were analogous to the renaming and reduction rules of the lambda calculus. In section 5 below we give a careful definition of entry to and exit from blocks and procedures which is

essentially a precise version of the semantics
given in the ALGOL report.

Semantic definitions of block structure languages in terms of literal substitution and copy
rules have a certain conceptual simplicity but are
computationally impractical. It has been shown by
Lucas [L4], Henhapl and Jones [H2] and Jones and
Lucas [J2] that a number of successively more
practical implementations of identifier accessing
in block structure languages are equivalent to the
definition in terms of literal substitution. The
structure of such proofs is further discussed in
[M10].

Proofs of interpreter equivalence are important
in proving that a practical (efficient) implementation is equivalent to the interpreter which constitutes the language definition. If A is the defining interpreter of a programming language, then
a proof of equivalence of B and A may be thought of
as a proof of correctness of B. Moreover, if C is
a third implementation of the language defined by
A, then C may be proved correct by proving its
equivalence to B. It is possible by means of a
sequence of proofs of equivalence of interpreters
to build up an equivalence class of interpreters
each of which is guaranteed to be a correct implementation of the language definition. The defining
interpreter A may be thought of as a representative
element of such an equivalence class.

Since interpreters are very complex objects,
it is by no means obvious how relations such as
equivalence and correctness between interpreters
should be formulated. Moreover, during the 1960s
there was an overemphasis on program syntax and
compilers at the expense of program semantics and
interpreters, which led to an overemphasis of the
notion of compiler correctness at the expense of
the notion of interpreter correctness. It will be
shown below that interpreters are a more central
class of phenomena in computer science than compilers
and that proofs of compiler correctness require a
proof of interpreter correctness as an essential

ingredient.

Although McCarthy [M3,M4] had introduced
models of interpretation as early as 1960, it was
not until the Vienna definition language had demonstrated the feasibility of defining interpreters for
complex programming languages [W2] that the interpreter equivalence problem for real programming-
language interpreters began to be seriously studied.
Thus the proofs of Lucas [L4] and Henhapl and Jones
[H2] constitute the first example of a group of
interpreter equivalence proofs which establish an
equivalence class of significantly different,
practically important interpreters.

In a parallel independent development, Wegner
introduced the comparative study of interpreters
of the lambda calculus [W3,W4]. Wegner's informal
studies were formalized by McGowan [M7,M8,M9] who
proved the equivalence of a number of significantly
different lambda calculus interpreters. Although
proofs of equivalence of lambda calculus interpreters are not as practically significant as proofs
of equivalence of implementations of block structure
languages, McGowan and Wegner, by studying a simpler
class of interpreters, were able to pay more attention to methodology [M10,W5]. The present paper
constitutes a further attempt to characterize the
methodology and significance of proofs of interpreter correctness.

5. A COPY RULE MODEL FOR IDENTIFIER ACCESSING

Block structure languages associate a charac-
teristic semantics with identifiers. Identifiers
are *bound variables* in the sense that all occurrences
of an identifier associated with a given identifier
definition* may be replaced by some other identifier

---

*An occurrence of an identifier is said to be a
defining occurrence when it occurs as the declared
variable of a declaration or as a parameter of a
procedure. All other occurrences of an identifier

without changing the "meaning" of the program. On
entry to a block a cell is created for each identifier declared in the head of the block, and instances of use of the declared identifier are interpreted as references to the cell. On entry to a procedure, each parameter called by value is interpreted as a reference to an initialized newly-created
cell, each parameter called by reference is interpreted as a reference to the cell associated with
the actual parameter in the calling environment,
and each parameter called by name has every instance
of use of the parameter initialized to the actual
parameter expression.

The semantics of bound variables with nested
scopes was first defined for the lambda calculus
[C2,C4]. The scope rules of the lambda calculus
were taken over by ALGOL 60 and other block structure languages. However, the semantics for identifier accessing given in the ALGOL report [N2] was
very different from the techniques of identifier
accessing used in implementations such as that of
Dijkstra [D2,R1].

In the present section, a semantics for identifier accessing is defined which generalizes the
semantics given in the ALGOL report to the case of
label and procedure variables, and makes precise
the rather vague statements in the ALGOL report
regarding "suitable systematic changes of the formal
or local identifiers." The relation between this
definition and practical implementations of identifier accessing is then considered in section 6.

The semantic model developed below will be
called the *copy rule model* since block and procedure
entry is accomplished by the creation of suitably

---

are said to be instances of use of an identifier.
The phrase "all occurrences of an identifier" denotes all occurrences bound by scope rules of the
block structure language to the defining occurrences
and excludes instances of the identifier symbol not
bound to the defining occurrence.

modified copies of the blocks and procedures being
entered. The semantics of the copy rule model will
be defined by an information structure model
(I, I^0, F). The principal features of the structures
I^0 and I are briefly considered, and the transformation rules for block entry, block exit, procedure
entry, procedure exit and goto statements are given.

Initial representations $I_0 \varepsilon I^0$ have the form
(ip_0, S_0, D_0) where ip_0 is the initial *instruction
pointer*, S_0 is the initial *stack component* and D_0
is the initial *denotation component*. The initial
stack component S_0 has a single entry (the entry
at level 0) containing a representation of the
program to be executed, the initial instruction
pointer ip_0 points to the first instruction of the
program, and the initial denotation component is
empty.

Execution-time states $I_j \varepsilon I$ have the form
(ip, S, D). The component S consists of a stack of
representations of partially executed program segments. The instruction pointer ip points to an
instruction in the top stack entry. The denotation
component contains cells created on entry to blocks
and procedures which may be accessed by cell names
substituted for occurrences of identifiers at the
time of cell creation. The denotation component
may contain cells of different types, where the
type of a cell is determined by the data type of the
declaration or specification which causes the cell
to be created.

The information structure transformations
associated with block entry may be defined as
follows:

Copy rule for block entry: On entry to a block,
allocate a cell in the denotation component for each
declared identifier, having the type specified by
its declaration.* Create a *new copy* of the *block*

---

*Declarations may be either initialized or unini-
tialized. In ALGOL 60, data declarations for integer, real and Boolean identifiers are uninitialized,

being entered with all instances of identifiers
declared in the block replaced by the cell names of
the corresponding newly created cells. Increase
the instruction pointer ip to point to the first
executable statement of the block.

The above copy rule is illustrated in Figure 1
below for an ALGOL 60 program consisting of a block
with an inner nested block. Statements of the program have been numbered so that they can be referred
to by the ip. It is assumed that on entry to a
block the statement numbers of statements of the
newly created block are the same as those of corresponding statements of the stack entry being executed
when the block was created.*

---

while declarations for identifiers of the type
"label" and "procedure" are initialized at block
entry time. It is here assumed that block structure
languages may contain procedure-valued variables p
to which values may be assigned by statements of
the form p='procedure body'. Procedure values are
stored in the denotation component as literal
strings of text in which identifiers non-local to
the procedure body are assumed to have been replaced
by cell names n_i of identifiers declared in an
enclosing block. Assignment of a procedure body
thus preserves the correspondence between non-local
procedure identifiers and the cells in the denotation
directory with which such non-local identifiers were
associated at declaration time. The data values
required to represent labels are even more complex
than those which represent procedures and are discussed below in describing the semantics of goto
statements.

---

*We have here interpreted the phrase "all instances
of identifiers declared in the block" as referring
only to instances bound by declarations. Thus the
inner bound instances of y are not bound by the
declaration of y in the outer block. An alternative
"renaming rule" which also renames inner stances
of y on entry to the outer block and then renames
them again on entry to the inner block would have
the same effect as the above rule.

```
ip→1: begin integer x,y;     ip─┐1: begin integer n₁,n₂;
   2:   x:=y:=0;                │2:   n₁:=n₂:=0;
   3:   begin integer y;      └→3:   begin integer y;
   4:     x:=y:=1;               4:     n₁:=y:=1;
   5:     y:=y+1;                5:     y:=y+1;
   6:   end;                     6:   end;
   7:   print(x,y);             7:   print(n₁,n₂);
   8: end;                      8: end;
```

Initial Program (ip=1)   First Copy (ip=3)

```
      ip─┐3: begin integer n₃;
         │4:   n₁:=n₃+1;
         │5:   n₃:=n₃+1;
         └→6: end
```

Second Copy (ip=6)[†]

(†An alternative to copying only the entered block would be to copy the complete program segment on block entry with suitable renaming of the entered block.)

Figure 1

Illustration of the Copy Rule for Block Entry

Exit from a block is accomplished by deletion of the copy of the block created on entry and continuing with the statement following the end of the block in the immediately preceding copy.

Rule for block exit: On exit from a block by execution of its *end* statement, delete the copy of the block whose execution has been completed. Increment the instruction pointer by 1 and execute the instruction determined by ip in the copy of the program segment being executed at the time of entry to the exited block.

The sequence of copies of program segments created on block entry and deleted on block exit is always created and deleted in a last-in-first-out order. The component S therefore forms a stack with respect to the creation and deletion of copies of program segments.

Block exit causes deletion of the block from the stack component but does not cause the deletion of cells from the denotation directory.

Retention rule for cells: Cells which are created on entry to a block are never deleted.

Cells which become inaccessible on block exit may, however, be deleted without changing the logical effect of a program. Garbage collection of inaccessible cells by a garbage-collection algorithm or even by a stack mechanism may be justified by a garbage-collection theorem.

Garbage-collection theorem: Cells which become inaccessible may be deleted without changing the logical effect of a program.

Proof: The logical effect of a program is completely defined in terms of execution-time information structure transformations. Since inaccessible cells cannot affect execution-time transformations, they may be deleted without changing the logical effect of the program.

The justification of cell deletion as a theorem rather than as part of the semantic definition is by no means obvious. ALGOL 60 was designed so that block exit always implied that cells created on entry to the block became inaccessible and could therefore be deleted. For more complex block structure languages like PL/I block exit does not necessarily imply that cells created on entry to the block become inaccessible, and failure to distinguish between block exit and cell deletion may in such cases lead to confusion. The distinction between block exit and cell deletion is further discussed in section 7 of [W6] and in [J1,B1].

The above definition of the semantics of block entry is the result of a long evolutionary process and much careful thought. Thus the rule for

avoiding naming conflicts was wrongly stated in the
original ALGOL 60 report [N1] and obscurely stated
in section 4.7.3.3 of the revised report [N2].
Incorrect interpretations of the semantics of
identifiers have given rise to numerous wrong implementations of macro languages, ALGOL 60, PL/I, and
have even resulted in a wrong definition of the
simple LISP APPLY function on page 13 of [M6].

This confusion in the field of programming
languages had its counterpart in mathematics where
numerous wrong definitions of substitution were
proposed in the 1920s before a correct definition
was developed by Church [C2] and Curry [C4] in the
1930s.

The above semantics for entry to and exit from
blocks has been carefully defined so that it can be
extended to procedures.

Formal parameters of procedures are similar to
declared identifiers of blocks in being bound
variables, but differ from declared identifiers in
the way in which they are initialized on entry to
a procedure. Whereas identifiers declared in blocks
are always bound to a newly created cell on block
entry, formal parameters of procedures are sometimes bound to a preexisting expression or cell
transmitted through the point of call. There are
three forms of initalization of formal parameters
to actual parameters, referred to respectively as
initialization by value, initialization by reference
and initialization by name. All three forms of
parameter initialization may be defined in terms of
a copy rule for procedure entry which creates a
suitably modified copy of the procedure with
instances of formal parameters replaced by structures which realize the appropriate parameter
initializations.

Copy rule for procedure entry: On procedure
call, create a copy of the procedure body in which
occurrences of formal parameters called by value,
reference and name are replaced by structures
described below which realize parameter initializa-

tion. Substitute for the termination symbol of the
procedure body the statement "return ip;" where ip
is the statement number of the statement following
the point of call.

Parameters initialized by value give rise to
the creation of a cell at procedure entry time,
initialization of this cell to an actual parameter
value, and replacement of all instances of the
parameter identifier in the body of the procedure
by the cell name n_i of the newly created cell.
Initialization by value has the same semantic effect
as an initialized declaration in a block head.

Parameters initialized by reference must be
initialized to actual parameters whose value is
the name n_i of a cell created prior to procedure
call. Initialization by reference causes all
instances of the formal parameter in the body of
the procedure to be replaced by copies of the cell
name n_i which constitutes the actual parameter value.
Initialization of a formal parameter x to a cell
name n_i causes sharing of the cell n_i by the parameter x and instances of n_i in the calling program.

The semantics of initialization by name may
be defined in terms of the replacement of all
occurrences of the formal parameter (other than the
instance of declaration) by a literal copy of the
expression which constitutes the actual parameter.
Thus if the parameter x of P(x) is initialized by
name, then a call P(a+b*c) would result in the
replacement of all instances of the formal parameter
x in the procedure body by copies of the expression
"a+b*c". Since all identifiers occurring in an
actual parameter expression such as "a+b*c" must,
by previous application of the copy rule for blocks
and procedures, have been replaced by cell names
n_i, the actual expression substituted is of the form
"$n_p + n_q * n_r$" where n_p, n_q, n_r are cell names
associated with particular instances of activation
of blocks and procedures rather than identifiers
of the static program.

Exit rule for procedures: Initialize the

instruction pointer to the ip of the "return ip" statement, pop the top entry in the stack of program segments, and continue execution at ip in the new top entry of the stack.

Procedure entry and exit may be illustrated by the simple example in Figure 2.

```
1: begin real x,y;              1: begin real n₁,n₂;
2:   procedure P(z);real z;     2:   procedure n₃(z);real z;
3:     begin                    3:     begin
4:       x:=z+1;                4:       n₁:=z+1;
5:     end;                     5:     end;
6:   y:=1;                      6:   n₂:=1;
7:   P(y*y);                    7:   n₃(n₂*n₂)
8: end                         8: end
```

```
3: begin
4: n₁:=n₂*n₂+1
5: return 8;
```

Figure 2

Illustration of the Copy Rule for Procedure Entry

The retention and garbage collection rules hold for procedure exit as well as block exit. Cells created on procedure entry are conceptually never deleted, but may in practice be deleted when they become inaccessible.

The language operators introduced above define the semantics of entry to and exit from blocks and procedures. In defining the semantics of goto statements, the representation of label data values must be considered. It is assumed that statement labels explicitly introduced by the programmer give rise in the compiled program to label declarations

in the innermost block enclosing the point of
declaration, and that label values may be freely
assigned to label-valued variables declared outside
the block of declaration of the label constant.
This gives rise to the problem that labels in program segments from which exit has occurred may still
be accessible because they have been assigned as
values of label-valued variables in outer blocks,
and that exit from a block should not therefore
cause program segments containing such labels to be
deleted.

The rule that exit from a block or procedure
always implies deletion of the corresponding program
segment may be salvaged by storing a complete copy
of the stack at the time of declaration as part of
the label value. Thus label values will have the
general form (ip,S) where ip is the statement number
of the labelled statement and S is a copy of the
stack component at the time of creation of the label
value. On entry to a block which contains a label
declaration the cell n_i created for the label value
is initialized to the value (ip,S), where S is a
copy of the stack after entry to the block of
declaration. On entry to a procedure, the value of
the return label is (ip,S) where S is the stack
before entry to the procedure.

The semantic effect of a goto statement may now
be defined as follows:

Goto rule: Execution of the statement "goto n_i;",
where the cell n_i contains a label value of the form
(ip,S), causes replacement of the current stack component by the stack component S and replacement of
the current instruction pointer by the instruction
pointer of the label value.

The above rule requires a complex and space-
consuming representation of labels. The data representation of label constants may, however, be
simplified when the following conditions are
satisfied:

   a)   the label constant cannot be modified

and cannot be assigned as the value
of a label variable;
b) the relation between the program
stacks before and after execution of
the transfer of control is known at
compile time.

Thus, if the statement "goto L;" is not separated by any block boundaries from the statement
labelled L. the stack after execution is guaranteed
to be the same as that before execution and the
statement "goto n_i;" with the associated value
(ip,S) in the cell n_i may be replaced by a simple
statement "jump ip;" where jump is an instruction
which replaces the ip component by its literal
parameter without modifying the data stack.

The statement "return ip;" substituted for the
terminating symbol of a procedure at procedure call
time may similarly be regarded as an abbreviation
of the statement "goto n_i;" where n_i contains the
value (ip,S) and S is a copy of the stack at the
point of procedure call.

Theorem: The procedure entry and exit rules
are equivalent to a modified procedure entry rule
in which "goto n_i;" with n_i initialized as above
is substituted in place of ip for the termination
symbol of the procedure, and procedure exit is
accomplished by execution of the goto statement.

Proof: The two techniques always result in
identical ip and stack components on exit from a
procedure.

The above theorem proves the equivalence of an
interpreter in which procedure return is implemented
by goto statements and a second interpreter in which
procedure return is implemented by a return instruction. The "goto n_i;" interpreter has fewer primitive instructions, while the "return ip;" interpreter
implements procedure return more efficiently. In
the next section a number of equivalent models of
block structure interpretation with much more
radical differences in execution-time organization

will be considered. Proof techniques for proving
the equivalence between the copy rule model and
more efficient interpreters will then be considered
in later sections.

6. IMPLEMENTATIONS OF THE COPY RULE MODEL

In the copy rule model the names n_i of cells
which contain data values are directly substituted
for identifiers before their execution. In actual
implementations the program being executed usually
remains invariant throughout execution and the cell
names associated with instances of execution of
identifiers must be accessed through symbol tables
(directories) or computed by an address computation
function. As a first step in simulating direct
substitution of cell names for identifiers by
indirect addressing we shall consider an implementation of parameter initialization by reference in
terms of initialization by value.

Rule for simulated initialization by reference:
On entry to a procedure create for each parameter x
called by reference a cell n_{new} and initialize n_{new}
to a copy of the cell name n_i which constitutes
the value of the actual parameter. Replace all
instances of x in the copy of the procedure body
by n_{new}. Whenever a parameter initialized by
reference is encountered, access the value of the
parameter by one-level indirect addressing.

Theorem: The rule for simulated initialization
by reference has the same semantic effect as the
rule for direct substitution of parameters n_i for
identifiers x.

Proof: Substitution for all instances of x of
a cell name n_{new}, initialization of n_{new} to n_i, and
use of an accessing rule which specifies that parameters initialized by reference are accessed by
one-level indirect addressing has the same semantic
effect as direct substitution for all instances of
x together with an accessing rule which specifies

that all instances of x are accessed by indirect addressing.

The device introduced above of simulating direct addressing by one-level indirect addressing may be used to simulate literal substitution for declared identifiers by one-level indirect address-ing of the cell name through an *environment* table of correspondences between identifiers and cell names.

Definition: The model described below in which all currently accessible identifiers may be accessed by one-level indirect addressing through an environ-ment table will be called the *complete environment model*.

Block entry in the complete environment model may be specified by the following environment creation rule:

Environment creation rule for block entry: On entry to a block, allocate for each declared identi-fier x a cell n_i of the type specified by its declar-ation. Create a copy of the "old" environment table of correspondences $(x:n_i)$ prior to block entry and superimpose on this environment table the newly-created set of correspondences $(x:n_i)$ determined by local declarations, *replacing* "old" entries having locally declared first components x by newly declared correspondences $(x:n_i)$ and *augmenting* the table with entries whose first component did not appear in the old environment table. Begin execution of the entered block using the new environment table to look up the cell names currently associated with identifiers.

The complete environment model is a *fixed program model* in the sense that the program being executed remains invariant throughout execution. Variation between identifiers and the cells which they denote during execution is represented in the copy rule model by substitution of cell names in a copy of the program and is represented in the complete environment model by a stack of symbol

tables which parallels the stack of program segments
of the literal substitution model.

Theorem: The environment creation rule for
block entry has the same semantic effect as the
copy rule for block entry.

Proof: There is a one-to-one execution-time
correspondence between copies of blocks created
by the copy rule and copies of environment tables
created by the environment creation rule. There is
also a one-to-one correspondence between cells
created by the copy rule and the environment creation
rule. At any given point of execution, occurrences
of a cell name n_i corresponding to an accessible
cell in the newly-created currently executing block
created by the copy rule will correspond to an
environment table entry (x,n_i) of the environment
created on entry to the corresponding block by the
environment creation rule. Direct accessing of the
cell n_i in the copy rule model may therefore be
simulated by one-level indirect addressing in the
complete environment model.

The complete environment model is a more
practical model of block entry than the literal
substitution model but is sufficiently similar to
the literal substitution model that it can easily
be proved equivalent. It was initially used by the
Vienna definition group as the basic definition of
block entry [L5]. However, in later language
definitions [W2] the literal substitution model
was used as the basic definition.

The complete environment model may be regarded
as a transitional model which simulates literal
substitution of references for identifiers by
symbol table lookup but nevertheless contains
features which are implemented more efficiently in
practical implementations. Two implementations
which have been proved equivalent to the complete
environment model by the Vienna definition group
are described below.

The *local environment model* as given by Lucas

[L5] simulates complete environment tables by a
linked list of local environment tables (corresponding to locally declared identifiers). The link
from a local environment table to a textually
enclosing local environment table corresponds to
the notion of a static link [R1,W3]. A proof of
equivalence of the local environment model and
complete environment model is given in [L4]. The
structure of this proof is further discussed in
[W7].

The *local denotation model*, which is essentially
a variant of the *display model* due to Dijkstra [D2],
dispenses altogether with environment tables for
storing cell names n_i associated with identifiers
x, and instead allows the current cell name associated with an identifier to be uniformly computed by
an *address computation function*. In order to
facilitate the address computation, identifiers are
replaced prior to execution by integer pairs (i,j)
where i is the static level of nesting of the point
of declaration and j is the relative address in a
local denotation table. Local denotations are
linked by a static chain just as local environments
of the local environment model. The group of local
denotations associated with a given instance of
execution of a block or procedure is called an
activation record.

The local environment model may be characterized
by an information structure model whose instantaneous
descriptions I have the form (ip,P,S_E,H) where ip is
an instruction pointer, P is the fixed program, S_E
is a stack of *local environments*, and H is the data
storage area (heap) in which components are retained
as long as there is an addressing chain originating
in the stack which points to the component. Each
local environment contains a set of correspondences
(x,n_i) between locally-defined identifiers x and
corresponding unique names n_i, and a *static link
component* n_S which specifies a textually enclosing
local environment. Identifier accessing of an
instance of execution of an identifier y in the
fixed program P is accomplished by looking for an
entry of the form (y,n_j) first in the current local

environment and then in successive textually enclosing local environments accessible via static chain
links n_s. The cell name n_j of the entry (y,n_j)
found in this way is then used to access the cell
associated with this instance of execution of the
identifier y.

The local denotation model may be characterized
by an information structure model whose instantaneous descriptions I have the form (ip,P,S_D,H) where
ip is an instruction pointer, P is the fixed program,
S_D is a stack of *local denotations* and H is the data
storage area (heap) for data structures with non-
local lifetimes [W6]. The local denotations in the
component S_D may be thought of as being constructed
from corresponding local environments in the component S_E by replacing entries of the form (y,n_i) by
denotations d_j contained in the cell n_j. The accessing rule by symbol table look-up along the static
chain used in the local environment model is replaced
by an accessing rule using a display of origins of
local denotation components [R1,W3]. Some of the
denotations of the component H of the local environment model are stored in the local denotation model
in the component S_D, thus saving space, accessing
time and garbage-collection time. The distinction
between local and non-local denotations is further
discussed in [W6].

In the local environment model, exit from a
block or procedure may be uniformly defined in terms
of deletion of a layer of the local environment,
and denotations are conceptually retained forever.
In the local denotation model, exit from a block or
procedure cannot in general be implemented by deletion of the local denotation, since there may be
references to data cells of the activation record
from program segments whose execution has not yet
been completed. The rule for exit from blocks and
procedures must therefore be much more carefully
defined for denotation models than for environment
models.

The detailed definitions and proofs of equivalence of a number of models of identifier accessing,

including those above, are given in [L4,H2,J2].
We shall consider below the structure of such proofs.

7. TWIN MACHINE PROOFS OF INTERPRETER EQUIVALENCE

Whenever two objects, say A and B, are to be
proved equivalent, there are certain features
which A and B have in common and certain differences
between A and B whose equivalence is to be proved.
A good proof of equivalence requires A and B to be
characterized in such a way that common features are
automatically factored out and that differences are
characterized in a way which suggests how the
equivalence might be proved.

More specifically, if A and B are each infinite
classes of objects (such as classes of computations)
then a finite representation of both A and B is
required which imposes a common inductive structure
on both A and B that may be used as the basis of an
inductive equivalence proof [W8]. Information
structure models emphasize the sequence of instructions executed rather than the static structure of
initial representations, and suggest an inductive
structure which allows us to perform our primary
induction on the sequence of instructions executed
rather than on the set of initial program states.
The twin machine proof technique described below is
essentially a technique for imposing a common
inductive structure on two classes of computations
(interpreters) which allows induction on corresponding sequences of executed instructions to be carried
through.

The general problem of whether two arbitrary
interpreters A, B are functionally equivalent is
clearly undecidable. However, in proving the equivalence of different implementations of identifier
accessing we are fortunate in that the class of
interpreters which need be considered is constrained
by very strong constraints. In particular, we may
assume that the two interpreters being proved
equivalent execute corresponding sequences of

instructions, and differ only in using different
mechanisms for accessing cells associated with
identifiers.

The above restrictions on the kind of differences which need be considered allow us to embed the
two interpreters being proved equivalent in a *twin
machine* which uses a single control mechanism for
executing the instruction sequence common to the
two computations but generates disjoint information
structures for realizing the different identifier
accessing mechanisms of the two interpreters.

Let $M = (I, I^0, F)$ and $M' = I', I^0', F')$ be the
two interpreters whose equivalence is being proved.

Define a twin machine $M'' = (I'', I^0'', F'')$ whose
information structures I'' contain components
corresponding to both M and M', and whose instructions combine the effect of execution of corresponding instructions in M and M'. In particular, M''
will contain information structure components for
implementing the methods of identifier accessing of
both M and M', and instructions for entry to and
exit from blocks and procedures which simultaneously
update the information structures required for the
two methods of identifier accessing. The twin
machine is assumed to automatically check at the end
of each executed instruction whether or not the two
methods of identifier accessing give rise to the
same next instruction. If during the execution of
a conditional branching instruction such as
"*if* x = 0 *then* ..." the two methods of identifier
accessing cause branching to different next instructions, the twin machine model will automatically
abort the computation.

The equivalence of M and M' may be defined in
terms of the condition that for any instance of
accessing of an identifier in M'', the cell accessed
by the identifier accessing mechanisms in M'' corresponding to M and M' is the same. Let $find_1(id, I_j)$
be an accessing function which computes the cell
name n_i for identifiers id accessible in the state
I_j of M'' by means of the accessing mechanism of M,

and is undefined otherwise. Let $find_2(id,I_j)$ be
the corresponding accessing function for M'. Then
the equivalence of M and M' can be defined in terms
of the functional equivalence of $find_1$ and $find_2$
in M".

Definition of interpreter equivalence: M is
equivalent to M' if and only if for all identifiers
id and states I_j of M", $find_1(id,I_j) = find_2(id,I_j)$.

In block structure languages the only operations
which cause the accessing environment to be modified
are block entry, block exit, procedure entry, procedure exit, and goto statements. The proof of
equivalence of identifier accessing developed in
[L4] proves that equivalence of accessing is preserved by block and procedure entry, and that block
exit, procedure exit and goto statements recreate
an accessing environment of the twin machine for
which the accessing equivalence has already been
proved. It is shown that for all initial states
I_0 of the twin machine $find_1(id,I_0)$ and $find_2(id,I_0)$
always yield the same result (the value undefined).
Induction is then used to show that if $find_1$ and
$find_2$ yield the same value for all identifiers id
prior to the execution of an instruction which
modifies the accessing environment, they will yield
the same value for all identifiers id immediately
after execution of that instruction.

The details of the proof procedure may be
found in the source literature [L4,H2,J2] and are
discussed from a tutorial point of view in [W7].

The above proof depends on the fact that the
two interpreters M and M' execute a corresponding
sequence of instructions and can therefore be
simulated by a single machine which performs the
common instruction sequencing of M and M' in a
single processing unit. This condition is met whenever the two interpreters being proved equivalent
are constrained to execute a common *fixed program*
and to differ only in the structures which they
generate during execution. However, the technique
is not limited to fixed-program interpreters. It

has been adapted by Henhapl and Jones [H2] to proving the equivalence of the copy rule (which requires
the program to be modified) to fixed-program methods
of identifier accessing.

A number of successively looser relations
between interpreters may be defined, each of which
is amenable to twin machine proofs.

1. *Fixed program interpreters* M, M' which
are guaranteed to execute the same fixed program
for corresponding computations and differ only in
the information structures generated during execution.

2. *One-to-one interpreters* M, M' which have
the property that there is always a one-to-one
correspondence between executed instructions
(execution sequences) of M and M', but which may
execute different program representations. The
literal substitution (copy rule) model and the complete environment model of identifier accessing
are related in this way.*

3. *Linearly related interpreters* M, M' which
have the property that subcomputations of M and M'
are performed in the same order, but which may have
a many-to-one or one-to-many correspondence between
instruction sequences required to perform specific
subtasks.

4. *Segment-wise related interpreters* M, M'
which have the property that corresponding segments
of M and M' can be defined such that there is a
one-to-one correspondence between the execution of
segments in M and M', but which may involve radic-
ally different computations within such segments.
In this case the twin machine technique may be used

---

*The literal substitution model executes instruc-
tions of *copies* of the program while the complete
environment model executes a single fixed program.
The creation of copies of the program in the literal
substitution model is performed by the "control" of
the "literal substitution machine."

to prove equivalence assuming the equivalence of
corresponding segments, and an independent proof
technique must be used for proving the equivalence
of corresponding segments.

The twin machine model works best for fixed
program interpreters. Although it may be adapted
to both one-to-one interpreters and linearly related
interpreters, these cases are better handled by the
mapping techniques discussed in section 10.

8. OUTPUT-EQUIVALENT INTERPRETERS

The twin machine criterion of equivalence of
implementations of identifier accessing defines a
special case of interpreter equivalence. We shall
define below a more general criterion of equivalence
called *output equivalence* which corresponds to the
intuitive notion of functional equivalence of two
interpreters. The relation between output equivalence and specific subcases such as twin-machine
equivalence will then be considered.

Two functions f_1, f_2 are said to be equivalent
if they have the same domain D and range R and define
the same rule of correspondence between elements of
the domain and elements of the range; i.e., if for
all $x \varepsilon D$, $f_1(x) = f_2(x) \varepsilon R$ and for all $x \notin D$ $f_1(x)$ and
$f_2(x)$ are undefined. We can extend the above notion
of equivalence to functions over different domains
and ranges.

Let $f_1:D_1 \to R_1$ and $f_2:D_2 \to R_2$ be functions with
respective domains D_1, D_2 and ranges R_1, R_2, and let
$\emptyset_D:D_1 \to D_2$ and $\emptyset_R:R_1 \to R_2$ respectively map the
domain and range of f_1 into the domain and range
of f_2. Then f_2 is said to *simulate* f_1 *under the
mapping* $(\emptyset_D, \emptyset_R)$ if and only if for all

$$\forall (x \varepsilon D_1) \; [\emptyset_R(f_1(x)) = f_2(\emptyset_D(x))]$$

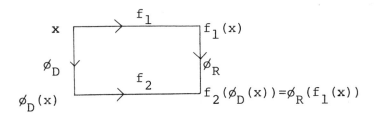

Figure 3

Commutative Diagram for the Equivalence of Functions
Over Different Domains

Definition: f_2 *simulates* f_1 if and only if there
exist mappings $\phi_D : D_1 \rightarrow D_2$ and $\phi_R : R_1 \rightarrow R_2$ such that

$$\forall \; (x \varepsilon D_1) \; [\phi_R(f_1(x)) = f_2(\phi_D(x))]$$

    Lemma: The relation f_2 simulates f_1 is re-
flexive and transitive.

    Proof: Reflexiveness follows from the fact that
that the relation "f_2 simulates f_1" is always
satisfied by choosing ϕ_D and ϕ_R to be identity
mappings. In order to prove transitivity, assume
that f_2 simulates f_1 under (ϕ_D, ϕ_R) and f_3 simulates
f_2 under (ϕ_D', ϕ_R'). Then f_3 simulates f_1 under
$(\phi_D' \cdot \phi_D, \phi_R' \cdot \phi_R)$ where $\phi_D' \cdot \phi_D$ is the composition of the
mappings ϕ_D', ϕ_D and the mapping $\phi_R' \cdot \phi_R$ is the composition of the mappings ϕ_R' ,ϕ_R.
    We shall be concerned with restrictions of the
relation "f_2 simulates f_1" defined by the following
condition:

    Symmetry Condition: The relation "simulates"
is symmetric; i.e., "f_2 simulates f_1" => "f_1 simulates f_2".

simulates f_1" is symmetric. This requires us to find an equivalence-preserving mapping ϕ_D^* which maps elements of a given computational equivalence class E_2 of the domain D_2 under $\equiv_{f_2}$ into elements of the computational equivalence class E_1 of D_1 under $\equiv_{f_1}$ which maps into E_2 under ϕ_D.† Such a mapping may always be defined by picking representative elements in each equivalence class of $\equiv_{f_1}$, and mapping all elements in a given equivalence class under $\equiv_{f_2}$ into the representative element of the equivalence class of $\equiv_{f_1}$ which maps under ϕ_D into the given equivalence class of $\equiv_{f_2}$.††

The above theorem allows the definition of mappings D between domains of source and target programs which map computationally equivalent expressions of the source language into given representative elements of the target language.

A criterion of output equivalence for

---

†The domain D_2 may include elements which cannot be obtained by the application of ϕ_D to an element of D_1. For example, if ϕ_D is a compiler, then there may be many programs in the target language which are not generable by the compiler but which are equivalent to a program generable by the compiler. The function ϕ_D^* must map all elements of D_2 into D_1 including those which are not the image of any elements of D_1 under ϕ_D.

---

††Although a mapping ϕ_D^* corresponding to the mapping ϕ_D always exists, there is no general algorithm for determining the ϕ_D^* associated with a given ϕ_D; i.e., ϕ_D^* cannot be expressed as an effective function of ϕ_D. However, for the purpose of establishing output equivalence it is sufficient to establish the existence of a "symmetric" mapping ϕ_D^*.

interpreters may be defined by analogy with the corresponding criterion for *functions*.

Let $M = (I, I^0, F)$ and $M' = (I', I^{0'}, F')$ be two interpreters, and let $\phi_D: I^0 \to I^{0'}$ be a mapping from initial representations of M to initial representations of M'. Let $I_T^0 \subseteq I^0$ be the subset of initial representations which determine terminating computations in M. Let "interpret$_M$" be the *interpreter function* for M which determines final representations when applied to initial representations of I_T^0 and is undefined otherwise, and let interpret$_{M'}$ be the corresponding interpretation function for M'. Let "output" be a function which selects output components of final representations of both M and M', and let ϕ_R be a one-to-one function which maps output components of M into output components of M'.

The interpreter M' is said to simulate the interpreter M under the mappings ϕ_D, ϕ_R and given output function if and only if the following conditions hold:

1. The computation determined by $I_0' = \phi_D(I_0)$ in M' terminates if and only if the computation determined by I_0 in M terminates.

2. For all final representations $I_n =$ interpret$_M(I_0)$ and $I_m' =$ interpret$_{M'}(\phi_D(I_0))$ we have output $(I_m' = \phi_R(\text{output}(I_n)))$.

The above definition of output equivalence is essentially a specialization of the notion of simulation for functions, as illustrated in Figure 4 below.

Definition: An interpreter M' is said to simulate

the interpreter M for a given output function on
final states if and only if there exists a mapping
ϕ_D from I^0 to $I^0{}'$, and a one-to-one mapping ϕ_R from
output components of M to output components of M'
which satisfies conditions (1) and (2) above.

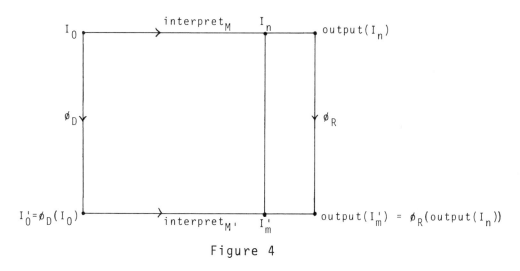

Figure 4

Commutative Diagram for the Simulation of an
Interpreter M by an Interpreter M'

        Lemma: The relation "M' simulates M" is reflex-
ive and transitive.

        Proof: The relation "M simulates M" is
satisfied when ϕ_D and ϕ_R are the identity functions.
If M' simulates M by (ϕ_D,ϕ_R) and M" simulates M' by
(ϕ_D',ϕ_R') then M" simulates M by $(\phi_D' \cdot \phi_D, \phi_R' \cdot \phi_R)$.

        The notion of output equivalence for interpre-
ters can be defined as a restriction of the relation

"M' simulates M".

Symmetry condition: The relation "M' simulates M" is symmetric; i.e., M' simulates M => M simulates M'.

Definition: If "M' simulates M" and the symmetry condition is satisfied, then the two interpreters M, M' are said to be output-equivalent.

Theorem: Output equivalence of interpreters is an equivalence relation.

Proof: The relation "output equivalence" is reflexive, transitive and symmetric.

We shall consider a number of alternative restrictions on ϕ_D for a one-to-one onto mapping ϕ_R.

Output mapping restriction: The output mapping ϕ_R is one-to-one onto.

Theorem: If "M' simulates M" and ϕ_D, ϕ_R are one-to-one onto mappings, then M and M' are output-equivalent.

Proof: The mappings $(\phi_D^{-1}, \phi_R^{-1})$ satisfy the relation "M simulates M'", so that the relation simulates satisfies the symmetry condition.

The notion of output equivalence may be extended to the case when ϕ_D is many-to-one by introducing the notion of computational equivalence classes over the domains $I^0, I^{0'}$ of M and M'.

Definition: Let $\equiv_M$ be the equivalence relation defined by an interpreter M on its domain I^0 which has the property that $x_1 \equiv_M x_2$ if and only if the initial representations result in computations with the same output component in the interpreter M.

This equivalence relation will be referred to as *computational equivalence*.

Definition: Let $\equiv_M$ and $\equiv_{M'}$ be computational equivalence relations for interpreters M,M' satisfying the relation "M' simulates M". The mapping ϕ_D is said to be an equivalence-preserving mapping if all elements in any computational equivalence class of M are mapped into the same computational equivalence class of M', and there is a one-to-one correspondence between equivalence classes of M and M' under the mapping ϕ.

Theorem: Let M, M' satisfy the relation "M' simulates M", let ϕ_R be one-to-one, and let ϕ_D be an equivalence-preserving mapping. Then M and M' are output-equivalent.

Proof: We must prove that if ϕ_D is an equivalence-preserving mapping then we can find an equivalence-preserving mapping ϕ_D^* for which "M simulates M'". Pick representative elements in each equivalence class of $\equiv_M$, and map all elements of a given equivalence class of $\equiv_{M'}$ into the representative element of the equivalence class of $\equiv_M$ which maps under ϕ_D into the given equivalence class of $\equiv_{M'}$. The choice of this mapping as ϕ_D^* and the choice of ϕ_R^{-1} as ϕ_R^* will automatically give us a mapping (ϕ_D^*, ϕ_R^*) for which "M simulates M'".

The above analysis of output equivalence will be briefly summarized and the reasons for choosing the particular definitions and restrictions will be indicated. The definition of output equivalence is defined by the following two-part relation:

a)   Definition of simulates:

$$\exists (\phi_D, \phi_R) \; \forall \; I_0 [M'(\phi_D(I_0)) = \phi_R(M(I_0))]$$

b)   Simulates is a symmetric relation.

Condition (b) may be replaced by the following sufficient but not necessary conditions:

b1) ϕ_R is one-to-one onto

b2) ϕ_D is one-to-one onto

The condition (b2) is in general too restrictive, since compiler mappings from a source to a target interpreter are often many-to-one. For example, in PL/I, programs containing abbreviations or default specifications are equivalent to completely specified programs. The following less restrictive condition is sufficient for output equivalence but less restrictive than (b2):

b2') ϕ_D is a many-to-one equivalence-preserving mapping.

The condition (b2') can be relaxed even further in the case of a many-to-many correspondence between source and target domains.

Definition: A binary relation R_D over $I^0 \times I^0$, which maps elements of computational equivalence classes of I^0 into corresponding computational equivalence classes of $I^{0'}$ will be referred to as an *equivalence-preserving relation*.

b2")   The correspondence between source and target domains is expressible as a many-to-one equivalence-preserving relation R_D.

The condition (b2") is appropriate when we wish to express the fact that any one of a number of computationally equivalent elements of the target language domain is equally acceptable as the image

of a given element of the source language domain.
Thus arithmetic expressions such as ((a*b)+(c*d))
may, in the absence of side effects, be mapped into
the equivalent postfix forms ab*cd*+ or cd*ab*+.
More generally, whenever it can be proved that
evaluation is insensitive to changes in the order
of evaluation of component expressions [S3] we may
wish to express equivalence under changes in the
order of evaluation in terms of a one-to-many
mapping condition (b2").

   The condition (b2") is appropriate also in
defining equivalence classes of parallel computations in terms of the class of all possible orders
of sequential evaluation. For example, the notion
of a control tree in the Vienna definition language
was introduced to allow the parallel specification
of subcomputations whose order of execution is not
defined by the programming language. The equivalence class of all sequential implementations to
which a given control tree can give rise could in
principle be defined by a many-to-one mapping (b2").

   The factoring of the definition of interpreter
equivalence into different parts focuses attention
on different attributes which we would like definitions of interpreter equivalence to have. Part (a)
focuses attention on the fact that if M is equivalent to M' then M' should be able to simulate M.
Part (b) reflects the fact that output equivalence
should be an equivalence relation, and parts (b1)
and (b2) represent restrictions on output and input
mappings which realize this equivalence relation.
Part (b1) restricts the mapping ϕ_R to be one-to-one
because interpreters whose equivalence it is desired
to prove almost always have a one-to-one correspondence between outputs. Conditions (b2), (b2'),
(b2") represent three successively more general ways
to implement the mapping between initial representations.

   The equivalence classes imposed on the domains
of M and M' by the relation of computational equivalence are not effective equivalence classes, since
it is not in general possible to determine for

arbitrary initial representations of M whether they
will yield the same value. However, the equivalence
relation imposed on the domains of M and M' by a
given equivalence-preserving mapping ϕ_D is generally
a refinement of the relation of computational equivalence for which it is decidable whether two initial
representations of M are mapped into the same
initial representation of M'.

The definition of interpreter equivalence
involves two different kinds of mappings:

1) Mappings of initial representations of the
interpreter into their values under interpretation.

2) Mappings of initial representations of a
source language interpreter into initial representations of a target language interpreter.

The first kind of mapping is an *irreversible*
mapping in the sense that computation is supposed to
be a unidirectional irreversible many-to-one mapping.
The equivalence classes of initial representations
which have the same value under interpretation are
generally non-effective.

The second kind of mapping is intended to be
reversible, as is shown by the trouble to which we
have gone to ensure that a reverse mapping exists.
The equivalence classes imposed on initial representations by a mapping ϕ_D are generally effective.

The study of the relation between non-effective
mappings imposed on a domain by an interpreter and
effective equivalence classes imposed on a domain
by compilation or other "syntactic" transformations
is common to many different models of interpretation.
For example, the reduction rules of the lambda
calculus impose a non-effective equivalence relation
on lambda expressions while renaming rules impose
an effective equivalence relation on lambda expressions.

Because interpretation is generally a non-
effective process while compilation is an effective

process, it is appropriate to consider the relation between interpreters and compilers in terms of an abstract model in which there is an asymmetry between the properties of irreversible non-effective interpretation functions and reversible effective compilation functions. However, once we have an abstract model in which function equivalence is defined by a commutative diagram, further abstraction may well result in the study of interpretation functions which are related by non-effective compilation functions.

Although the definition of output equivalence in terms of the conditions (a), (b) above is a specialization of the general notion of function equivalence, it nevertheless determines a *weak* and therefore *general* definition of interpreter equivalence. Stronger forms of interpreter equivalence may be defined both by specialization of condition (b) to conditions (b1) and (b2), (b2') or (b2") and by specializations which impose a relation on intermediate states of interpreters being proved equivalent. Thus, twin machine equivalence is an example of a form of interpreter equivalence that is a specialization of output equivalence.

Definition: Two interpreters are said to be *twin-machine equivalent* if their equivalence can be proved by the twin machine proof technique (described in section 7).

Theorem: Interpreters which have been proved equivalent by the twin machine proof technique are output-equivalent.

Proof: The correspondence between instruction sequencing required for the twin machine proof to go through guarantees that computations of the two interpreters being proved equivalent terminate for precisely the same elements of their domain. The equivalence relation which is proved to hold for all intermediate states of a twin machine proof holds also for final states and guarantees that one interpreter simulates the other. Symmetry of the proof technique guarantees that the relation simulated is

an equivalence relation. A one-to-one mapping
function ϕ_R is not directly implied by the twin
machine proof technique, since the technique as
such is concerned with mappings between intermediate
states of the interpreter rather than the interpreter. However, a suitable output function can always
be chosen with respect to which the mapping ϕ_R is
one-to-one.

Corollary: The relation of twin-machine equivalence is a *refinement* of the relation of output
equivalence in the sense that interpreters which have
been proved twin-machine equivalent are always output-
equivalent while interpreters which are output-equivalent are not necessarily twin-machine equivalent.

Proof: Two deterministic interpreters in which
the order of two independent subcomputations is
interchanged are output-equivalent but not twin-
machine equivalent.

Output equivalence is a *non-constructive* definition of equivalence in the sense that the equivalence criterion does not suggest a specific proof
technique for proving interpreter equivalence.
Twin-machine equivalence may be regarded as a special
case of output equivalence which, by virtue of the
fact that it assumes a correspondence between intermediate states of the computation, suggests a proof
technique for verifying the equivalence of interpreters.

It is in principle possible to develop a large
number of proof techniques each of which is associated with a class of interpreters provably equivalent
under that proof technique. The equivalence classes
of interpreters which can be proved equivalent in
this way form a lattice. The points of this lattice
represent *semi-constructive* equivalence classes* in

---

*The term semi-constructive is used because the class
of interpreters which can be proved equivalent by a
given proof technique is not necessarily an effective
equivalence class. For example, there is no algorithm for determining whether or not two arbitrary

the sense that each lattice point is associated with a proof technique for proving equivalence. The class of output-equivalent interpreters is a non-constructive equivalence class which is a least upper bound of the lattice of semi-constructive equivalence classes.

One of the tasks of further research in interpreter equivalence is to develop semi-constructive proof techniques which are more powerful than the twin-machine technique and which at the same time imply output equivalence.

9.   INFIX AND POSTFIX EXPRESSION EVALUATION

The twin-machine technique works best when the interpreters being proved equivalent are guaranteed to execute the same fixed program. We shall refer to this special case of twin-machine equivalence as *fixed-program equivalence*.

Although the twin-machine proof can be adapted to proofs of equivalence for one-to-one interpreters and linearly related interpreters, it is often unnatural to force such proofs into the twin-machine mold. A proof technique due to McGowan is described below which focuses attention on the *mapping* between corresponding or linearly related states of the interpreters being proved equivalent. This allows direct comparison of complete states at corresponding points of a computation without imposing the intermediate step of embedding corresponding states in a twin machine.

---

interpreters are twin-machine equivalent. However, proof techniques such as the twin-machine technique suggest the recasting of the problem into a form which emphasizes a particular kind of inductive structure. Once the problem has been recast into this form the applicability of the proof technique may generally be determined by examining the structure of the interpreters to be proved equivalent.

The structure of proofs using the mapping technique will be illustrated by considering the equivalence between infix and postfix evaluation of a simple class of arithmetic expressions, and the generalization of this proof technique to the lambda calculus will be briefly indicated.

Consider a simple class of fully parenthesized arithmetic expressions defined by the following syntax:

$$E \rightarrow I \mid (E+E) \mid (E*E) \quad \text{where I is the set of integers}$$

The semantics of this class of expressions may be defined by the following semantic evaluation rule:

Reduction rule for infix expressions: Find any subexpression of the form (i+j) or (i*j) where i and j are integers and replace it by its value.

Example: The expression ((3*4)+(5*6)) may be evaluated by reducing the subexpressions (3*4) and (5*6) to their value in either order, and then reducing the subexpression (12+30) to its value.

Mathematicians have traditionally written arithmetic expressions in infix notation and it is mathematically appropriate to define arithmetic expression evaluation directly in terms of trans- formations on infix strings. However, infix evaluation is non-deterministic in the sense that there may be more than one expression of the form (i+j) or (i*j) which can be evaluated at any given time. Moreover, the discovery of a reducible subexpression involves a relatively complex pattern- matching operation. From a computational point of view it is simpler to represent the operators and operands of an arithmetic expression in *postfix* form, using the following syntax:

$$E \rightarrow I \mid EE+ \mid EE*$$

Postfix expressions such as 34*56*+ may be thought of as instruction sequences which are executed from left to right. Operands are copied into an operand data stack S while operators are applied to the two top operands in the operand stack. Execution of postfix strings may be defined with the aid of an instruction pointer ip which points to the next executable symbol of the postfix string and a data stack pointer dp which points to the first free cell of the data stack. The expressions P(i), D(i) respectively denote the ith element of the program string and data stack, while |P| denotes the number of instructions in the program string.

F = if ip > |P| then D(1)
    else if P(ip) = operand then
      [D($\overline{dp}$):=P(ip);dp:=dp+1;ip:=ip+1;]
    else if P(ip) = operator then
      [D($\overline{ip}$-2):=apply(P(ip),D($\overline{dp}$-2),D(dp-1));
                          dp:=dp-1;ip:=ip+1;]
    else error

This model of postfix evaluation has more complex information structure components than the previously described infix model, since it has a program component P, a data stack component D, and the pointer components ip and dp. Moreover, the transformation rule for infix evaluation may be more simply stated than the corresponding rule for postfix evaluation. However, postfix evaluation may be carried out by the sequential execution of a sequence of operator and operand symbols, and constitutes a computationally more appropriate definition of expression evaluation than the conceptually simpler infix definition.

Since the infix definition was historically first and is, from the mathematical point of view, a simpler definition, it is reasonable to regard the infix model of expression evaluation as the basic definition and to regard the postfix model as a derived model whose correctness must be

justified by proving its equivalence to the infix
model.

    The equivalence of the postfix and infix inter-
preters may be proved with the aid of a mapping
function $\emptyset$ from states of the postfix model to
states of the infix model. The function $\emptyset$ may be
defined recursively as a function which performs a
sequence of mappings each of which modifies the
data stack and increases the component ip.

$\emptyset$(D,ip) = <u>if</u> ip > |P| <u>then</u> D(1)
    <u>else</u> <u>if</u> P(ip) = operand <u>then</u>
     $\overline{\emptyset([\overline{P(ip)}:D]}$,ip+1)
    <u>else</u> <u>if</u> P(ip) = operator <u>then</u>
     $\overline{\emptyset([\overline{S2}}$ P(ip) S1): REST],$\overline{ip+1}$)
      <u>where</u> D = [S1:S2:REST]
    <u>else</u> <u>error</u>;

    The function $\emptyset$ is structured similarly to F.
It terminates with the value D(1) when ip > |P|.
The component P(ip) is placed on the data stack if
it is an operand. However, if P(ip) is an operator
then the operator-operand combination (S2 P(ip) S1)
is constructed and placed on the stack, whereas F
applies the operator to its operands. Thus $\emptyset$
replaces the *application* of operators to operands
by the *construction* of an infix subexpression from
its postfix constituents.

    In the case of arithmetic expression evaluation
both the evaluation process and the mapping process
take the same number of steps and are guaranteed to
terminate. However, for more general operator-oper-
and languages such as the lambda calculus the application of operators to operands may lead to arbitrarily long computations for which the termination
problem is undecidable, while a syntactically-
driven mapping function has decidable attributes
which can be proved by structural induction over
the syntactic structure of states. The equivalence
of linearly related interpreters whose intermediate
states are related by a mapping function $\emptyset$ may be

proved by showing that $\emptyset$ has certain attributes, independently of the fact that computations of each of the interpreters being proved equivalent may have an undecidable termination problem.

Instead of directly proving the equivalence of the above infix and postfix interpreters, we shall consider some general properties of mapping functions between interpreters, and then show that the equivalence of infix and postfix interpreters is a special case of a more general theorem.

10.   THE McGOWAN MAPPING TECHNIQUE

In section 8, a number of restrictions of output equivalence were introduced and characterized in terms of restrictions on the mapping function $\emptyset_D$ between the domains of the computations being proved equivalent. In these definitions it was assumed to be against the rules to consider mappings between intermediate states in defining semantic equivalence, since the "meaning" of a computation was assumed to be determined by a functional relation between inputs and outputs independently of how the function was computed. However, from the operational point of view, it is precisely the process of moving from an initial to a final computational state that is of interest. The operational meaning of functional relations is defined in terms of equivalence classes of interpretation strategies for moving from initial to final states. The operational point of view thus leads to the definition of specializations of output equivalence in terms of mappings between intermediate states of the computations being proved equivalent.

Let $M = (I,I^0,F)$ and $M' = (I',I^0{}',F')$ be two deterministic interpreters, and let $\emptyset:I \rightarrow I'$ be a mapping from states of M to states of M'. In the present section we shall be concerned with the relation between successive states I_j,

$$I_{j+1} = F(I_j)$$

of the source model and corresponding images
$\emptyset(I_j), \emptyset(I_{j+1})$ in the target model. In section 8,
such terms as many-to-one and many-to-many were
used to describe a relation on initial representations determined by $\emptyset_D$. In the present section, the
mapping $\emptyset_D$ is, for purposes of simplification,
assumed to be strictly one-to-one, so that attention can be focused on many-to-one and many-to-many
relations between successive states of a source
computation and corresponding successive states of
a target computation.

For example, the mapping $\emptyset_D$ from initial states
$I_0 = (C_0, P_0, D_0)$ of the postfix interpreter in
section 9 onto infix expressions is one-to-one, but
the mapping $\emptyset$ from states $I_j = (C, P, D)$ of the postfix interpreter onto the infix interpreter is many-
to-one, since a state I_{j+1} obtained from I_j by the
execution of an operand instruction maps onto the
same infix expression as I_j.

A relation between interpreters M and M' will
be defined which, intuitively, guarantees that the
two interpreters perform subcomputations in the
same order and that progress in a computation on
one interpreter will, in a finite number of steps,
result in a state whose mapping represents progress
in the other interpreter. This relation is called
linear relatedness.

Definition: Two deterministic interpreters M =
(I, I^0, F) and M' = $(I', I^0{}', F')$ are said to be linearly
related if and only if there is a mapping function

$\emptyset : I \to I'$ between states of M and M' which satisfies the following conditions:

1)   The mapping $\emptyset$ is a one-to-one mapping of initial states of M onto initial states of M'.

2)   Let I_j be a non-final state of M and $I_k' = \emptyset(I_j)$ be a corresponding state of M'.   Then there is a finite $q \geq 0$ such that $\emptyset(I_{j+1}) = I_{k+q}'$. That is, a single computational step in M corresponds to at most a finite number q of computational steps of M'.

3)   If $\emptyset(I_j) = I_k'$ and I_k' is not a final state, then there is a finite $p \geq 1$ such that $\emptyset(I_{j+p}) = I_{k+1}'$. That is, at most a finite number of computational steps of M are required to advance one computational step in M'.

4)   If $\emptyset(I_j) = I_k'$ and I_k' is a final state then there is a finite $p \geq 0$ such that I_{j+p} is a final state and $\emptyset(I_{j+p}) = I_k'$.

5)   If I_j is a final state and $\emptyset(I_j) = I_k'$ then there is a finite $q \geq 0$ such that I_{k+q}' is a final state and $\emptyset(I_j) = I_{k+q}'$.

It can be shown that linear relatedness of two interpreters implies output equivalence.

Theorem: If two interpreters $M = (I, I^0, F)$ and $M' = (I', I^0{}', F')$ are linearly related, then they are output-equivalent.

Proof: Conditions (4) and (5) imply that computations in M terminate if and only if computations in M' terminate. Conditions (4) and (5) together with condition (1) imply that for all $I_0 \varepsilon I_T^0$, interpret$_{M'}$($\phi(I_0)$) = ϕ(interpret$_M$(I_0)).   Moreover, if ϕ is a mapping satisfying conditions (1) through (5) then the reverse mapping from the target to the source model also satisfies conditions (1) through (5).   The conditions (1) through (5) define a relation "M simulates M'" which is symmetric.   M and M' are therefore output-equivalent.

The above definition of linear relatedness is more general than necessary for many practical interpreter equivalence proofs, including the proofs of equivalence of infix and postfix expression evaluation and proofs of equivalence of different implementations of the lambda calculus.   It is sufficient in this case to restrict the mapping from M to M' to be many-to-one instead of many-to-many. The relation between M and M' when ϕ is many-to-one will be called "M is many-to-one on M'".   This relation may be defined as follows.

Definition: An interpreter M is said to be many-to one on an interpreter M' if and only if there is a mapping $\phi : I \rightarrow I'$ between states of M and M' which satisfies the following conditions:

1')   The mapping ϕ is a one-to-one mapping of initial states of M into initial states of M'.

2')   Let I_j be a non-final state of M and $I_k' = \phi(I_j)$ be a corresponding state of M'.   Then the successor state I_{j+1} of M is mapped under ϕ into either I_k' or I_{k+1}'.

3')   If $\phi(I_j) = I_k'$ and I_k' is not a final state then there is a finite $p \geq 1$ such that $\phi(I_{j+p}) = I_{k+1}'$.

4')   If $\phi(I_j) = I_k'$ and I_k' is a final state, then there is a finite $p \geq 0$ such that I_{j+p} is a final state and $\phi(I_{j+p}) = I_k'$.

5')   If I_j is a final state of M then $\emptyset(I_j) =$
I_k' is a final state of M'.

Corollary: If M is many-to-one on M' then M
and M' are output-equivalent.

Proof: Each of the five conditions defining
"M is many-to-one on M'" is a special case of the
corresponding condition for linear relatedness, so
that being many-to-one implies linear relatedness
and therefore output equivalence.

Theorem: The postfix interpreter of section 9
is many-to-one on the infix interpreter.

Proof: The mapping $\emptyset$ satisfies conditions (1')
through (5') required by the definition.

Corollary: The postfix and infix interpreters
of section 9 are output-equivalent.

The many-to-one mapping is required in mapping
infix evaluation onto postfix evaluation, since
the postfix interpreter requires instructions to be
executed for occurrences of both operators and
operands, while the infix interpreter executes only
as many instructions as there are operators in the
expression being evaluated. In fact, the finite
integer p which satisfies condition (3') may be
arbitrarily large since for any fixed p it is always
possible to find an arithmetic expression with more
than p operands preceding the first operator. Thus
a strengthening of condition (3') requiring p to be
uniformly bounded independently of I_j would not
allow the proof of equivalence of postfix and infix
interpreters to go through.

In the case of arithmetic expression evaluation
the mapping function $\emptyset$ is as complex as the interpreter M which defines postfix expression evaluation.
However, when the mapping technique is generalized
to proofs of equivalence of interpreters of the
lambda calculus, the complexity of the interpreter
increases so that the termination and computational
equivalence problem for states of the interpreter

becomes undecidable, while the complexity of the mapping function $\emptyset$ remains the same.

In proving the equivalence of complex objects it is important to define equivalence in terms of a relation that expresses the difference between objects being proved equivalent so that the complexity of the proof depends on the degree of difference between objects rather than on the inherent complexity of the objects being proved equivalent. The mapping technique allows us to systematically focus on differences between classes of objects expressed in terms of the mapping required to map objects in one class into corresponding objects of the other class. Such a mapping is useful both at the formal level in indicating the proof structure for a particular equivalence proof and at the intuitive level in factoring out interesting relations while ignoring irrelevant complexity.

Before leaving this section still another relation between interpreters will be introduced which is more general than linear relatedness and may be regarded as a half-way house between linear relatedness and input-output relatedness.

Definition: An interpreter M is said to be segment-wise related to an interpreter M' if and only if there is a partial mapping $\emptyset : I \rightarrow I'$ between states of M and M' which satisfies the following conditions:

1") The mapping $\emptyset$ is a one-to-one mapping of initial states of M onto initial states of M'.

2") and 3")   If I_j is a non-final state of M and there exists an $I_k' = \emptyset(I_j)$ which is a non-final state of M' then there exist integers $p \geq 1$, $q \geq 1$ such that $I_{j+p} = \emptyset(I_{k+q})$.

4")   If $I_k' = \emptyset(I_j)$ is a final state of M' then there is a finite $p \geq 0$ such that I_{j+p} is a final state of M and $\emptyset(I_{j+p}) = I_k'$.

5") If I_j is a final state of M and $\phi(I_j) = I_k'$ then there is a finite $q \geq 0$ such that I_{k+q}' is a final state and $\phi(I_j) = I_{k+q}'$.

It can be shown that segmentwise relatedness implies output equivalence.

Theorem: Two interpreters M, M' which are segmentwise related are output-equivalent.

Proof: M simulates M', and the relation is symmetric.

If M and M' are segmentwise related then there are reference points $I_k' = \phi(I_j)$ and $I_{k+q}' = \phi(I_{j+p})$ for which there is synchronization between the two interpreters. However, no assumption is made regarding the relation between interpreter states between such reference points. In the limit, when the only reference points are the beginning and end of the computation, this definition reduces to output equivalence.

11. McCARTHY'S MODEL OF SEMANTICS

McCarthy [M3] discusses with remarkable insight the relation between mathematics and a mathematical science of computation. He indicates that logical systems are designed to prove metatheorems about systems rather than theorems within specific systems, and that "Gödelization" of a language, while sometimes helping in the proof of metatheorems about the language, makes it much more difficult to prove that specific classes of expressions in the language have certain properties.

McCarthy indicates that we need a metalanguage for programming languages which reflects the

structure of expressions in the language, introduces
the metalanguage of recursion equations for specifying computations, and introduces the principle of
recursion induction for proving the equivalence of
computations specified by recursion equations. The
principle of recursion induction states that two
functions which satisfy the same recursion equation
have the same value for all elements in the domain
of the recursion equation. This principle allows
us to infer the equivalence of execution of two
functions on the basis of the fact that they may be
represented by the same normal form in a specific
metalanguage.

McCarthy may be thought of as the founder of
the operational approach to computational semantics.
His definition of LISP by the LISP APPLY function
constitutes the first semantic definition of a
function in terms of an interpreter, and has served
as the model for subsequent attempts to define
functions in terms of their interpreters. In [M3]
he makes an explicit commitment to the operational
approach in stating that "the meaning of a program
is defined by its effect on the state vector," and
lays the basis of subsequent descriptive and formal
operational models of programming languages by
introducing the notion of abstract syntax and giving
a semantic definition of a simple class of arithmetic expressions which has served as a prototype for
operational semantic definition of more complex
languages.

The McCarthy and Painter proof of compiler
correctness appeared initially to be a breakthrough
in the theory of computation, since it held out the
promise that nontrivial proofs of correctness of
practical programming systems which would guarantee
the absence of system bugs were only just around
the corner. Yet instead of stimulating a large
amount of similar activity, the McCarthy and Painter
proof appeared for a number of years to be the
pinnacle of this direction of research, and remained
a solitary example of proofs that system programs
have certain attributes. The reasons for the failure
of attempts to apply the McCarthy and Painter

technique to practical programming systems are examined below.

McCarthy and Painter were very ambitious in choosing to prove the correctness of complex programs such as compilers rather than of simpler programs such as summation or sorting programs. In order to reduce the complexity of their proof of compiler correctness, they chose a very simple class of arithmetic expressions as the source language.

Even in this simple case the definition of the source and target language and of the compiler are quite complex. The reader who wishes to understand the details of the proof must invest a great deal of time in order to understand the definitions before he can understand the details of the proof itself. However, the structure of the proof may be understood by a careful analysis of the relation between compilers and interpreters and of the way in which inductive techniques are used in proving that infinite classes of structures have certain properties.

A compiler may be thought of as a program which translates initial representations of an information structure model $M = (I, I^0, F)$ into the initial representations of a second information structure model $M' = (I', I^{0'}, F')$. A proof of compiler correctness must show that for all initial representations $I_0 \varepsilon I^0$ in M, translation by the compiler to an initial representation I_0' followed by a computation on I_0' in M' is output-equivalent to a computation on I_0 in M. Thus compiler correctness may be characterized by the commutative diagram shown in Figure 5 below.

The condition for compiler correctness may be stated as follows:

$$\forall I_0 \varepsilon I_T^0 \ \text{output}(\text{interpret}_{M'}(\text{compile}(I_0))) =$$

$$\text{compileresult}(\text{output}(\text{interpret}_M(I_0)))$$

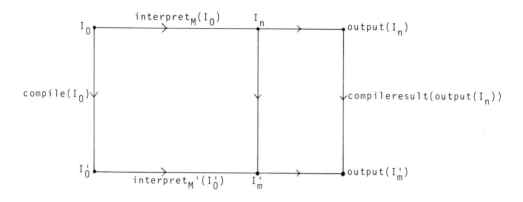

Figure 5

The Structure of a Proof of Compiler Correctness

This definition is merely an adaptation of the definition of output equivalence given in section 8 to the case of compilers.

The language for simple arithmetic expressions considered by McCarthy and Painter has a number of special properties. In particular, each syntactic constituent (operator or operand) is executed precisely once, and a one-to-one correspondence may be established between syntactic constituents of the source program and execution-time states of the source and target interpreters.

The proof of compiler correctness is accomplished by structural induction on the set of initial representations of the source language. The compiler is proved correct for constants and variables, and it is then proved that correctness of the compiler for the operands of an arithmetic expression implies correctness of the compiler for the operator-operand combination. This proof makes use in an essential way of the correspondence between syntactic constituents and execution.

The difficulty in extending the McCarthy and

Painter proof to compilers for languages whose
programs contain loops and conditional branching
was due in part to the fact that the original proof
contains no explicit mechanism for induction over
execution-time states. An analysis of Figure 5
indicates that proofs of compiler correctness must
prove the equivalence of execution for corresponding
programs in the source and target language. Two
distinct levels of induction are therefore required
in proofs of compiler correctness.

1. Induction over the set I^0 of initial representations of the source language model M. This
set may be defined by a syntactic notation such as
BNF which structures the infinite set of elements
of the set I^0 so that induction may conveniently
be performed and so that syntactic subcases in the
inductive proof correspond to semantic subcases.
The syntactic structure places certain constraints
on the sequence of execution-time states, but cannot in general provide sufficient information about
the structure and sequence of execution-time states
to prove assertions about the correctness and termination of computations.

2. Induction over the sequence of instantaneous descriptions generated during the execution of
a given program. This form of induction is much
more subtle than induction over structure components
of a syntactic definition, and it is not always
possible to find an inductive definition which allows
us to prove that all sequences of instantaneous
descriptions generable by a given information structure model posses certain attributes. McCarthy's
principle of recursion effectively states a sufficient condition over initial representations which
guarantees that an inductive proof over intermediate
states of the computation always goes through.
However, there are other ways of proving assertions
over intermediate states of the computation which
are more suggestive of the induction variables that
must be used in proving assertions about sequences
of execution-time states.

The set of all sequences of states generable

by a given information structure model may be represented by a two-dimensional array whose general
element I_{ij} represents the jth state of the ith
computation, as in Figure 6.

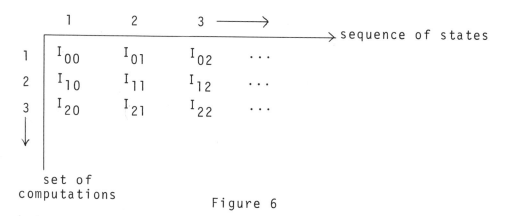

Figure 6

The Set of All Sequences of States of
An Information Structure Model

The first column of this array represents the
set of all initial representations and may be
inductively defined to facilitate inductive proofs
over elements of the set. In proofs of compiler
correctness it is tempting to use the inductive
structure over initial representations as the
primary inductive structure and to attempt to prove
assertions about sequences of computational states
by a subinduction for syntactic cases.

However, the induction problem over sequences
of states is harder than that over the set of initial
representations and there are advantages to considering this induction problem directly without being
encumbered by preconceptions about syntactic structure. For example, a proof that some or all of the
operators F of an information structure model preserve certain attributes of states whenever they

are executed considers the relation between a given
state and its successor without making explicit use
of the syntactic structure of states.

Induction over sets of initial representations
may be thought of as syntactic induction while
induction over sequences of states may be thought
of as semantic induction. The induction used in
the McCarthy and Painter proof of compiler correctness may be characterized as syntactic induction
(structural induction [B4]), while the induction
used in the twin-machine and mapping-technique
proofs may be characterized as semantic induction.

McCarthy realized the importance of defining
the meanings of programs in terms of their effect
on the computational state. His model of Microalgol
[M4] illustrates how a nontrivial programming language can be defined in terms of transformations of
a state vector. The Vienna definition group was
able to develop a synthesis of the semantic models
represented by LISP and Microalgol by introducing
the notion of a highly structured state whose components represented not only data values associated
with programmer-defined identifiers but also symbol
tables, pointers and other structures needed to
define a complete implementation of production programming languages. This in turn led to a formalism
for the descriptive characterization of execution-
time states of complex programming languages and
to proofs that programming language implementations
which generate highly structured states have certain
properties.

One of the most important contributions of the
subsequent work of the Vienna definition group was
to generalize McCarthy's model so that relations
among components of a highly structured state could
be explicitly considered, both at the descriptive
and the formal level.

12. FLOYD'S MODEL OF SEMANTICS

Floyd in [F2] is concerned with assigning meanings to programs rather than programming language interpreters. A program is represented by a program graph (flowchart) in which statements are represented by vertices and flow of control between one statement and the next is represented by a directed edge. A program graph has a distinguished input edge and a distinguished output edge. The semantics of a program P is defined by associating with each edge of the flowchart of P a predicate which specifies the set of all states that may obtain when control passes along that edge of the flowchart. The predicate associated with the input edge defines the domain of the program while the predicate associated with the output edge defines the set of all output states which may occur when the program terminates.

The semantics of a programming language is defined by a set of vertex types corresponding to instruction types. Each vertex type is characterized by a fixed number of inputs and outputs, and is defined by a relation (verification condition) which defines the state at each output edge as a function of the input states. The verification condition allows us to draw inferences about the state after an instruction has been executed from a knowledge of the state before the instruction has been executed.

A program of a given programming language is represented by a flowchart constructed from vertex types belonging to that programming language together with a mapping from edges of the flowchart into predicates which satisfy the verification condition of individual vertex types. However, the above class of programs can be embedded in a larger class of flowcharts in which the mapping from edges of the flowchart into predicates may be arbitrary. A flowchart of this larger class is said to be *consistent* if for each vertex the predicate at each output edge may be inferred from the predicates at input edges by the verification condition of that instruction type.

In applications programming we are often given a functional relation between inputs x and outputs y = f(x), and asked to write a program which realizes this functional relation. Floyd's flowchart notation provides a normal form for the representation of such programs which is not perhaps the most convenient for the programmer but is convenient for verifying whether the program correctly computes the function specified by a given relation between inputs and outputs.

Definition: A given flowchart correctly computes the program y = f(x) if the following conditions are satisfied.

1) We can associate a predicate $\phi(x)$ with the input edges which is true for all elements in the domain of f.

2) We can associate with the output edge the predicate $\forall(x\varepsilon\phi(x))\exists y[y=f(x)]$.

3) We can associate predicates with all other edges so that the flowchart is consistent.

If we are given a relation y = f(x) and wish to develop a program realizing this relation which is guaranteed to satisfy the above correctness criterion, we can go about it in one of the following ways:

a) Write a program in a user-oriented language which appears to realize the program and verify its correctness by "translating" it into the Floyd flowchart form.

b) Develop the program and the predicates associated with the edges of the flowchart in parallel, as suggested by Hoare [H3].

c) Use an algorithm for synthesizing an automatically correct program from its functional specification, as suggested by Manna and Waldinger [M2].

We shall analyze the inductive procedures
required in proving program correctness for a
program which has already been written and then
compare these inductive techniques with the techniques required to prove interpreter equivalence.

A proof of program correctness using the Floyd
technique requires induction at two levels:

1. In associating predicates with intermediate
edges of a program an inductive assumption is required about the form of the predicate associated
with at least one edge in each loop. This inductive
assumption must then be verified by showing that the
predicate holds on initial entry to the loop
(initial induction step), and that the execution of
the loop preserves the predicate (if it holds for n
executions of the loop it holds for n+1 executions).
This form of induction is required in order to
translate programs written by the user into the
form required by Floyd for correctness proofs. It
has been pointed out by Hoare [H3] and others that
the form of predicates at intermediate edges of
the flowchart can usually be determined relatively
easily since such predicates are essentially a
formalization of the programmer's intuitive reasoning in writing the program.

2. Induction to show that loops terminate for
all initial states which satisfy the predicate at
the input edge. A sufficient condition for this
induction to go through is to find a variable within
the loop whose sequence of values belongs to a well-
ordered set with a least element. Induction to
verify that the program terminates involves an
assertion about the *sequence* of values taken by a
variable while induction to verify that a predicate
is satisfied whenever control passes along a certain
edge involves an assertion about the *set* of all
instances that control passes along that edge.

Floyd's technique has been successfully used
to prove the correctness of programs which realize
a well-defined relation between inputs and outputs,
but does not appear to be suited to proofs of

correctness of programs such as interpreters for which the domain of termination is non-effective.

The Floyd correctness criterion has the following form:

$$\forall(x \in \text{Domain})\ \exists y\ [y = \text{value}(x)]$$

The complexity of this correctness predicate depends both on the complexity of the domain of x and on the complexity of the function "value." Moreover, the form of this predicate implies the existence of a y for all elements in the domain of x and breaks down when the domain of x is non-recursive. Floyd's notion of correctness is inapplicable to programs with an undecidable termination problem and some other correctness criterion must be used for such programs.

Interpreters are an important class of program with an undecidable termination problem. The correctness criterion used in twin-machine proofs and mapping proofs is different from the Floyd criterion and may be expressed by the following predicate:

$$\exists \phi \forall(I_j \in I)\ [\phi(M(I_j)) = M'(\phi(I_j))]$$

where ϕ is a function whose domain and range is the state set I and M, M' are the source and target language interpreters.

The above correctness criterion differs from the Floyd correctness criterion in the following important respects:

1) The Floyd criterion is a first-order formula of the predicate calculus while the second criterion is a second-order formula since the existentially quantified variable ϕ is a function over the domain

of the universally quantified variable I_j.

2) The Floyd criterion has the form $\forall x \varepsilon y P(x,y)$ while the second criterion has the form $\exists y \forall x P(x,y)$. The first form requires the existence of a possibly different y for every element of x while the second form merely requires the existence of a single y which satisfies $\forall x P(x,y)$. The second form is clearly easier to work with although in the present case the greater simplicity of form is balanced by the fact that the y whose existence is required is a function over x.

3) The variables over which universal quantification is performed have a different role in the two models. Moreover, the universally quantified variable of the Floyd model (the set of all inputs for which an output exists) has a non-recursive domain while the universally quantified variable of the second model has a domain which is a subrecursive superset of the set of all states arising in the computation.

4) The inductive structure required to prove equivalence for the two correctness criteria above is entirely different. The relation between required inductive structures for the two correctness criteria is examined further below.

In order to compare the inductive structures imposed on computations by an information structure model and a flowchart it is interesting to consider again the two-dimensional array of states associated with a computation (see Figure 7 below) where row i represents the ith computation and I_{ij} represents the jth state of the ith computation.

An information structure model uniformly represents computations by potentially infinite linear sequences and suggests induction on the jth state of all computations or alternatively induction on attributes of the state transition function F.

A flowchart groups together states associated with each edge of the flowchart. The states I_{ij}

	col 0	col 1	col 2	
Row 0	I_{00}	I_{01}	I_{02}	...
Row 1	I_{10}	I_{11}	I_{12}	...
Row 2	I_{20}	I_{21}	I_{22}	...

Figure 7

Differences of Inductive Structure Between
Floyd Predicates and Information Structure Proofs

grouped together by a single predicate may be widely
and irregularly scattered in the two-dimensional
array of Figure 7. The predicate may in many cases
express a natural grouping of instantaneous descriptions from a functional point of view. However, it
is clear that the way in which elements of the two-
dimensional array are mapped onto the finite number
of edges of the flowchart involves a radical reorg-
anization of the inductive structure. The inductive
structure of the flowchart replaces induction over
primitive transformations of the programming language by induction over loops occurring in specific
programs, thus tailoring the proof technique to the
particular program about which a result is to be
proved. However, when a proof is concerned with
attributes of classes of programs such as the class
of all programs of a programming language, then a
proof technique based on induction over primitive
transformations of the programming language is more
appropriate. Moreover, if the assertion that we
wish to prove is independent of program termination,
then the predicate used in proving the assertion
must not be restricted to programs which terminate.

A proof of correctness of a program P using
the Floyd technique uses as its correctness criterion a relation between program inputs and program

outputs, and requires induction over the flowchart
of the program P to prove the correctness. A proof
of equivalence of two programs P_1 and P_2 requires
two correctness proofs which respectively perform
an induction over the structure of the programs P_1
and P_2. The complexity of a proof of equivalence
of P_1 and P_2 depends on the complexity of P_1 and P_2
rather than on the complexity of the mapping between
P_1 and P_2.

In proving the equivalence of two objects P_1
and P_2 it is in general possible to use two classes
of proof techniques:

a) The normal form technique: Define a normal
form for the class of objects to which P_1 and P_2
belong and determine whether P_1 and P_2 are equivalent by comparing their normal forms.

b) The direct mapping technique: Determine
a mapping function which maps P_1 onto P_2 (or P_2
onto P_1) and show that this mapping function preserves the equivalence condition being proved.

The normal form technique has the advantage
that it provides a uniform proof procedure for all
objects in the class to which P_1 and P_2 belong,
while the direct mapping technique requires a
special mapping to be found for each pair of objects
P_1, P_2 being proved equivalent. However, when the
objects P_1 and P_2 are very similar and the normal
form to which P_1, P_2 are to be reduced is very
different from both P_1 and P_2 then it is worth
using the direct mapping technique.

The mapping from a program P to a normal form
defined in terms of a functional relation between
inputs and outputs depends on the complexity of the
program. When the program P is an interpreter or
compiler, this mapping is in general very complex,
and proofs of correctness which require this mapping
to be carried through are correspondingly complex.

In proving the equivalence of linearly related
interpreters we have a classic case of programs P_1,

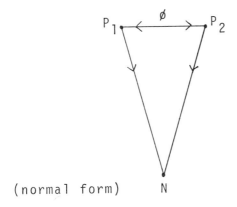

(normal form)   N

Figure 8

Relation Between Direct Mapping And
Normal Form Mapping

P_2 which are very complex but at the same time very
similar. The Floyd technique is in this case not
appropriate because the mapping of such programs to
a functional normal form would require a great deal
of work while the direct mapping of one program
into the other may be simply accomplished.

Interpreters are programs whose termination
problem is undecidable so that the mapping of an
interpreter P_1 onto the Floyd normal form is non-
effective. Thus an attempt to prove the equivalence
of two interpreters by proving the functional
correctness of each of the interpreters in terms of
a predicate which defines the relation between
inputs and outputs is not only difficult but theo-
retically impossible.

When we are concerned with relations between
objects such as interpreters that are very complex
but very similar, the proof technique should depend
not on the complexity of the objects for which the
relation is being proved but only on the differences between the objects. Thus the complexity of a
proof that two identical interpreters are equivalent

should be independent of the complexity of the interpreters.

In order to factor out the difference between complex objects as the primary factor of variation in a proof technique the assertion to be proved by the proof technique should have the following form:

∃ difference ∀ (corresponding elements E)

$$P(E,difference)$$

I.e., the assertion should start with an existential quantifier having a specification of the difference between the complex objects as its explicit variable.

In the mapping technique the mapping ∅ between interpreter states is a specification of the differences between interpreters, and the predicate calculus formula which characterizes the proof technique has precisely the form suggested above.

13. THE PREDICATE CALCULUS WITH ASSIGNMENT, EQUALITY AND CONTROL

The notion of model building and of relations among classes of models has been extensively studied in mathematical model theory, and some of the results of model theory are relevant to the development of computational models. The distinction between uninterpreted and interpreted models is one such notion.

Expressions of mathematical languages such as the predicate calculus consist of symbol strings whose constituents may have a fixed interpretation or an interpretation that varies over a specific domain. For example, formulae of the predicate calculus contain logical symbols (propositional connectives and quantifiers) which have a fixed interpretation and algebraic symbols (function and

constant symbols) which may have a variable interpretation. The formulae of the predicate calculus
are said to be *uninterpreted* if logical symbols have
a fixed interpretation, constant symbols are
unspecified elements of an unspecified domain and
function symbols are unspecified functions over the
domain of constants. The formulae of the predicate
calculus are said to be *interpreted* if constant
symbols are interpreted as specific constants of a
specific domain and function symbols are interpreted
as specific functions over the domain.

The term "uninterpreted" is misleading since it
suggests that all symbols of the language are uninterpreted. In fact, logical symbols have a fixed
interpretation even in an uninterpreted formula and
constant and function symbols are strongly constrained in the interpretation they may possess,
even though this interpretation is variable.

We may in general define a whole spectrum of
models of a mathematical language such as the predicate calculus which differ in the interpretation
constraints placed upon individual symbols. A
symbol with a fixed interpretation has an exception-
ally severe constraint placed upon its domain of
interpretation which forces it to have a unique
interpretation while a symbol with a variable interpretation has less severe constraints placed upon
its domain of interpretation. The class of all
interpretations of a given language forms a lattice
whose partial ordering relation is the inclusion
relation over systems satisfying the interpretation
associated with lattice points.

The predicate calculus with equality is an
example of a specialization of the general predicate
calculus in which the algebraic equality symbol is
given a specific interpretation while other algebraic symbols are allowed to vary over the same
constrained values as in the general predicate
calculus.

The purpose of fixing the interpretation of some
symbols while allowing the interpretation of others

to vary is to study attributes of the symbols
having a fixed interpretation while quantifying over
symbols having a variable interpretation. Thus
logical symbols of the predicate calculus have a
fixed interpretation because it is the properties
of these symbols that we wish to study. When it is
desired to study the properties of specific function
symbols over specific domains, we may further
specialize the model and fix the interpretation of
the function symbols and constants that we wish to
study.

   One advantage of systematically controlling
the domain of interpretation of the language we
wish to study is that it allows us to factor out
the study of attributes of specific symbols in a
systematic manner, and to introduce modelling
features associated with progressively more specific
classes of objects in a controlled manner.

   The above model-theoretic approach has been
applied to the development of models in computer
science by Manna [M1]. Manna uses a variant of
Floyd's flowchart model as a normal form for programs
and introduces a distinction between uninterpreted
and interpreted programs which parallels that of the
predicate calculus. The relation of Manna's model
to classical models of mathematical model theory
[T1,M11] will be briefly indicated, and the relation
of Manna's model to the operational models of semantics discussed in previous sections will be considered.

   Manna [M1] defines a normal form for programs
in terms of flowcharts which have program statements
as well as predicates associated with edges of the
flowchart. A predicate is called a valid predicate
for a given edge if it holds whenever control passes
along the edge and the statement associated with
that edge has just been executed, and is called a
minimal valid predicate for a given edge if only
states which can occur after execution of the statement at that edge are included in the predicate.

   Manna associates with each program a set $\bar{y}$ of

input variables and a set $\bar{x}$ of program variables, and assumes that each program statement consists of an assignment of values to program variables. If there are n program variables, then the program statement at a given edge may be represented by an n-tuple $(t_1,t_2,\ldots,t_n)$ where t_i, $i=1,2,\ldots,n$, are expressions of the programming language. Each edge also has associated with it a test predicate $\phi(\bar{y},\bar{x})$ which specifies the conditions that must be satisfied for control to pass along that edge.

An abstract program (uninterpreted program) is defined to be a program in which algebraic constant symbols and function symbols of the test predicate $\phi(\bar{y},\bar{x})$ and the expressions $(t_1,t_2,\ldots,t_n)$ may respectively vary over an unspecified domain and over unspecified functions of the domain of constants, as in the predicate calculus. An interpreted program is one in which the constant symbols are interpreted as specific constants, variable symbols are interpreted as variables over the domain of constants and function symbols are interpreted as specific functions over the domain of constants.

Manna's abstract programs associate a fixed interpretation with logical symbols and with the algebraic equality symbol just as in the predicate calculus with equality. However, since the purpose of Manna's model is to study certain computational phenomena this model associates a fixed interpretation also with certain computational primitives. In particular, a fixed interpretation is associated with the assignment operator by virtue of the form assumed for program statements, and a fixed meaning is associated with transfer of control statements by virtue of the fact that transfer of control is indicated by the fixed structure of the flowchart rather than by transfer of control functions with a variable meaning.

Since Manna's abstract programs superpose a fixed interpretation on assignment and control operations in addition to the fixed interpretation imposed by the predicate calculus on logical symbols and algebraic equality, this model may, from a mathematical point of view, be referred to as *The predicate calculus with equality, assignment and control.*

Manna's formalization of Floyd's model allows us to study properties of a fixed interpretation of certain transfer of control and assignment operators for a domain of variation of certain other symbols of programming languages. Moreover, it allows us to introduce in a controlled manner specific interpretations for certain function symbols. But, because it fixes the interpretation of transfer of control operators by representing them in a special notation, it does not easily generalize to other kinds of control operators such as procedures, co-routines, etc.

Manna's use of the predicate calculus as a primitive base for expressing semantics illustrates the difficulties of using mathematical notation for expressing the operational semantics of specific programming language implementations. The predicates and functional relations used by Manna in defining program semantics are expressed entirely in terms of symbols occurring explicitly in the program, and do not appear to encourage differentiation between execution-time structures generated by different implementations. Thus test predicates are expressed in terms of input and program variables, assignment functions are expressed in terms of assignment of values of programmer-defined expressions to program variables, and predicates defining the set of execution-time states associated with a given edge are defined in terms of the subset of permitted values of program variables at that edge.

The models of Floyd and Manna are intended to assign meaning only to programs and not to implementations of programs. This reflects the fact that the mathematical notion of interpretation is concerned only with the functional effect of symbols of a static program and deliberately does not distinguish between different implementations of the functional effect of program symbols. The predicate calculus with equality, assignment and

control is not intended to study differences of
implementation among interpreters, since it has
deliberately factored out differences at this level
in order to study "representation-independent"
attributes of programming languages.

From an operational point of view, representation-independent attributes of programming languages
should be justified in terms of information structure models that define meaning in terms of execution-time transformations generated by primitive
instructions. Attempts to define specific programming languages axiomatically generally obscure the
"natural" implementation-oriented semantics in terms
of which the language was conceived by its designers.
Indeed, we can go even further and say that, from
an operational point of view, there is no such thing
as the "meaning" of a program. Programs have a
meaning only insofar as we can characterize their
transformational effect during execution. Certain
programs which do not have a meaning when semantics
is defined in terms of a relation between inputs
and outputs have a well-defined meaning when
semantics is defined in terms of the execution-
time transformations to which the program gives
rise.

14. SOME OBSERVATIONS ON SEMANTIC MODELLING

Further insight into the relation between
Floyd's model of semantics and information structure
models of semantics may be obtained by comparing
Floyd's model with *fixed-program* information structure models such as the contour model [J1]. In
fixed program models, states are represented by snapshots consisting of an *algorithm* which corresponds
to Floyd's flowchart and a *record of execution* which,
in the context of Floyd's model, may be thought of
as a way of representing states associated with
instances of execution of edges of the flowchart.

A fixed program interpreter may be generatively
defined by specifying a generative transformation

rule which for any state I_j defines how the next
state I_{j+1} may be generated. Such a generative
definition allows us to generate the sequences of
snapshots which occur during the execution of any
given program. Generative definitions do not,
however, require the set of all states associated
with a given point of execution of the static
algorithm to be specified. This requirement is a
consequence of the inductive structure imposed on
computations by Floyd's model. The structure
imposed on computations by grouping together the
set of all states associated with a given point of
execution of the static algorithm is useful in
carrying out certain kinds of inductive proofs but
is inappropriate in other contexts.

In characterizing a class of objects such as
the class of computations performed by a given
program, we generally single out certain features
as *primary features* (primary keys of a classification) and consider other features only in terms of
the structure and classification imposed by primary
features. Floyd's model chose control structure as
the primary feature in classifying computations
associated with a program, and as a result considers
relations among data structures only after an
initial structuring has been imposed on the class
of computations being modelled. This form of
structuring is appropriate when control structure
can be used as the basis of inductive arguments to
prove assertions with which we are concerned. However, in the case of twin-machine proofs or mapping
proofs we have deliberately factored out the control
sequencing in order to study relations among data
structures independently of control sequencing. In
such cases it becomes appropriate to characterize
the class of computations determined by a program
in terms of primary features which emphasize data
structures generated during execution without
giving undue emphasis to control structures.

Information structure models use data structures
as the primary key for classification, and control
structures become one of a number of computational
attributes which may be defined in terms of data

structures.* Loops and predicates associated with
points of execution within a loop become abstrac-
tions which may in certain instances be defined in
terms of data structure primitives. Data structures
appear to be a more basic set of primitives for the
uniform characterization of classes of computations
than flowcharts, since flowcharts imply that control
structures are the primary key for classification
of computations, and impose an inductive structure
on program representations that is not always appropriate for proving the assertions in which we are
interested. Unannotated flowcharts are always
appropriate as a representation of the program
algorithm but annotated flowcharts are not always
appropriate as a representation of the meaning of
programs.

An information structure model specifies a
generative semantics for a class of computations
in terms of a generating rule for specifying
successive snapshots. In contrast, the mathematical
semantics of programs is generally defined by a set
of axioms or a correctness criterion which specifies
the necessary and sufficient behavior for an object
to be considered an instance of the given program.
The relation between generative and mathematical
semantics is, in some respects, analogous to the
specification of sets by a generator or a recognition criterion. Just as recognizers may be implemented by automata, so definitions of restricted
classes of computations in terms of a correctness
criterion may be implemented by a verification
algorithm [K1]. However, since semantic computational objects have an inherently more complex structure than syntactic computational objects, there
is a correspondingly larger gap between a mechanical
generative definition and devices for the mechanical
recognition of a correctness criterion, so that it
is usually necessary to bring the user into the

---

*Thus a "goto" command may be regarded as an assign-
ment of a label value ((ep,ip) pair) [W6] to the
processor while a procedure call creates and
initializes a new activation record and assigns a
label value to the processor.

verification process for the purpose of making
inductive assumptions.

At the syntactic level the relation between
generatively defined sets and sets defined by
recognition algorithms is not entirely symmetrical.
Historically, Chomsky's first mechanical models of
natural language were defined by generative algorithms [C1], and the generative models of Chomsky
were adopted as defining syntactic models for early
programming languages like ALGOL 60 [N2]. However,
a generative model of language is appropriate only
for the programmer who creates expressions of the
language and not for the computer which has to
recognize expressions generated by the programmer.
Computer-oriented models of syntax are more appro-
priately specified by a recognition algorithm. The
need to specify languages by recognition algorithms
led to the development of recognition-oriented
classes of grammars such as precedence grammars
[F3], bounded-context grammars [F4,I2], LR(k)
grammars [K2] and property grammars [S3].

At the semantic level the relation between
generatively defined semantics and recognition-
oriented semantics is even less symmetrical than
for the syntactic case. Generative semantics models
both hand-execution of a program and program
execution by computer. In the syntactic case the
generative model is appropriate to the construction
and transmission of messages while the recognition
model is appropriate to the receiving of messages.
In the semantic case the generative model is appropriate to the modelling of program execution and the
result of one execution step serves as the starting
point of the next execution step. Although a
recognition step is required as part of each generative execution step, there is no operational
reason to consider an operational semantic model
which is the symmetrical counterpart of the generative model. However, at the theoretical level, the
notion of a process that is the inverse of program
execution is interesting, and leads to models of
interpreters which may run backwards in time.

Asymmetry between syntax and semantics arises
in many different contexts. It arises at the
mathematical level in that compilers are generally
effective programs which halt for all inputs while
interpreters have an undecidable halting problem.
At the semantic level this asymmetry expresses
itself in a difference between modelling techniques
appropriate to syntactic recognition and semantic
execution. In developing formal proof techniques,
the asymmetry expresses itself by the fact that
computational equivalence between initial representations and their values is handled differently from
equivalence between source and target representations
under the mapping function $\emptyset$. However, although
there is an asymmetry in practice, it is possible
in each case to develop a symmetrical theory and to
regard the asymmetrical theory as a special case of
the symmetrical theory.

Practical computer professionals have for a
number of years felt that theoretical models of
computation such as those of automata theory and
formal languages were not relevant to practical
problems of programming. Conversely, theorists felt
that the consideration of practical problems led too
quickly to problems of unsolvability. Thus much of
the work in theoretical computer science has been
concerned with the characterization of subrecursive
sets. The books by Ginsburg [G1], Hartmanis and
Stearns [H1] and Hopcroft and Ullman [H4] represent
important syntheses of results concerning subrecursive sets. A recent paper by Constable and Borodin
[C3] identifies subrecursive classes of programming
languages so that they can be characterized by the
strong theorems applicable to subrecursive sets.
The work on subrecursive sets has yielded a great
deal of insight into the phenomena of computing.
However, it may well be that theoretical computer
scientists will increasingly turn their attention
to the study of properties of recursively enumerable
sets which arise in the characterization of interpreters and digital computers.

The reluctance of theorists to consider practical computational models may be due as much to

the fact that classical mathematical models are
inappropriate tools as to the inherent intractabi-
lity of such models. In particular, classical
mathematical models were *set-oriented* rather than
sequence-oriented. The failure to explicitly characterize the sequence of execution-time states
implicit in a program specification led to an undue
concern with syntactic questions. Models which
place greater emphasis on the sequence of execution-
time states may allow adequate mathematical models
of semantics to be developed.

It is important not to confuse the complexity
of the objects being studied with the complexity
of the relations that are to be proved about the
class of objects. Thus if A and B are complex
objects such as interpreters, there are many interesting tractable relations R(A,B) among such objects
which are worthy of study.* The equivalence of A
and B is an example of a relation which, in many
important cases, turns out to be both tractable and
practically important.

The study of hierarchies of tractable relations
over classes of recursively enumerable objects is a
mathematical problem area which may well become
computationally important. The lattice of equivalence relations over interpreters considered in the
body of this paper is an example of an interesting
hierarchy of relations over an important class of
non-recursive computational phenomena.

Certain relations among computational objects

---

*If A and B are objects having an undecidable
correctness or termination problem and the equivalence of A and B is provable, then, if an "oracle"
tells us that A is correct, we can deduce that B is
correct. However, the equivalence of A and B is
independent of the existence of oracles. It is
important to distinguish between the existence of
oracles for deciding undecidable questions and
relations over objects with unsolvable decision
problems which remain valid independently of the
existence of an oracle.

A and B may sometimes be proved to imply other
relations. The following type of theorem, which is
further discussed in [W5], might become important
in the study of computational semantics.

$$\text{For all } A,B \varepsilon C, \; R_1(A,B) \implies R_2(A,B)$$

For example, if R_1 is the relation of twin
equivalence over interpreters and R_2 is the relation
of output-machine equivalence, then for all interpreters A,B; $R_1(A,B) \implies R_2(A,B)$.

From an operational point of view, it is
important to classify relations in terms of their
verifiability. We have introduced the notion of a
constructive relation as a relation which is not
necessarily effective, but whose structure is such
that a proof technique for verifying the relation
is suggested by examining the definition of elements
of its domain. Whereas the notion of effectiveness
(decidability) of a relation is determined by
representation-independent properties of elements
in the domain of the relation, the notion of con-
structiveness is determined by a specific defining
mechanism for a class of objects. A relation may
be constructive with respect to one defining
mechanism and not constructive with respect to
another defining mechanism. This point of view is
in line with the operational attitude that meaning
is to be associated not with Platonic abstract
objects but with observable attributes of a specific
defining mechanism of a class of objects.

15. LANGUAGE DEFINITION BY SEMI-CONSTRUCTIVE INTERPRETER EQUIVALENCE CLASSES

We have advocated an operational approach to
semantics which leads to the definition of programming languages in terms of their interpreters. The
definition of a programming language by a specific

interpreter is somewhat restrictive when contrasted
with the axiomatic approach which defines programming languages in terms of axioms constituting
necessary and sufficient conditions for the correctness of an interpreter. However, if we have at our
disposal a set of proof techniques for proving the
equivalence of interpreters, then we can associate
with any given interpreter the equivalence class of
interpreters which can be proved equivalent to it.
A definition of a programming language by a specific
interpreter gives rise to a derived definition in
terms of the equivalence class of provably equivalent
interpreters which is much less restrictive than the
basic definition but is at the same time firmly
operational.

    For example, if PL/I or ALGOL 68 is defined
using a literal substitution model for identifier
accessing, then the twin-machine technique associates
a class of equivalent interpreters with the basic
definition including the complete environment model
and the Dijkstra display model. The knowledge that
there is a spectrum of equivalent interpreters is
practically useful and forms a basis for the formal
definition of the language in terms of an equivalence class of interpreters.

    Output equivalence appears to be the natural
formalization of the intuitive notion of equivalence.
However, there is no general decision procedure for
determining whether two interpreters are output-
equivalent. Moreover, the criterion of output
equivalence does not suggest any constructive procedure whereby this correspondence might be proved.

    Specific proof techniques such as the twin-
machine technique or the McGowan mapping technique
guarantee sufficient but not necessary conditions
for output equivalence, and define equivalence
relations over classes of interpreters that are
refinements of the output equivalence relation.
Such equivalence relations are special cases of the
general intuitive notion of equivalence but have
the advantage that the equivalence classes can be
constructively characterized in terms of a proof

technique for proving interpreters equivalent. The
resulting equivalence classes still are not
decidable since there is no decision procedure for
determining whether arbitrary interpreters may be
proved equivalent by a proof technique. However,
the equivalence classes will be called *semi-constructive* since necessary and sufficient conditions
for equivalence are determined by a constructive
criterion.

From the point of view of the implementer it
may often be more useful to define programming
languages in terms of semi-constructive equivalence
classes of interpreters for which the equivalence
relation is defined in terms of provability by
certain proof techniques rather than in terms of
non-operational axiomatic definitions. This allows
us to avoid tying a programming language definition
too closely to a specific implementation while at
the same time keeping careful control over what we
are prepared to regard as equivalent, and maintain-
ing a rigorous criterion as a basis for language
definition.

One of the objectives of semantic modelling is
to develop proof techniques which further enlarge
the equivalence class of provably equivalent interpreters. It is here conjectured that whenever there
is a strong intuitive basis for interpreter equivalence a proof can be developed which is either a
special case of an existing proof technique or an
instance of a new proof technique that enlarges
the class of provably equivalent interpreters.
Thus, when a system programmer comes up with a new
ingenious way of implementing a programming language
construct, he usually has a strong intuitive reason
for believing that his implementation is equivalent
to implementations which are known to be correct.
These intuitive reasons can generally be formalized
into an interpreter correctness proof which either
verifies the correctness of the intuition or shows
up some bugs which require the new impelmentation
to be modified or scrapped.

Although interpreters are generally very

complex programs, interpreters which are conjectured to be equivalent to each other generally bear a
strong initial resemblance to each other which can
be made use of in developing an interpreter equivalence proof. Thus, although the general problem
of equivalence for arbitrary interpreters is
undecidable, the equivalence of interpreters in
whose equivalence we are practically interested may
generally be proved or disproved.

The operational approach has both *practical*
advantages in expressing equivalence directly in
terms of information structure transformations
which are of concern to the implementer and
theoretical advantages in defining semantics in
terms of observable attributes of mechanisms which
realize programming languages rather than in terms
of independently developed abstract notions. The
theoretical advantages of an operational approach
should not be underestimated. In physics it was
found that the systematic application of operation-
alism led to the replacement of certain "Platonic"
notions of models of Newton, Lagrange and Laplace
by operational notions of relativity and quantum
theory. In computer science it is similarly
important to regard operational notions derived
from realizable models as the basic raw material
for the construction of theories, and to regard
non-operational axiom systems as secondary constructs
which must be justified by their correspondence with
operational models before they can be used with
confidence.

The definition of programming languages in
terms of semi-constructive equivalence classes of
provably equivalent interpreters may perhaps turn
out to be a compromise between Platonic and operational approaches to the semantic definition of
programming languages which satisfies both the
implementer and the theoretician.

ACKNOWLEDGEMENTS

I should like to thank Dan Berry and Clem McGowan for patiently reading earlier drafts of the manuscripts and keeping my philosophical extravagances within bounds, and Trina Avery for her superb typing.

REFERENCES

B1   Berry, D.M., "Introduction to Oregano," Symposium on Data Structures in Programming Languages, *SIGPLAN Notices*, 1971.

B2   ——, "Block Structure: Retention or Deletion?," 3rd SIGACT Symposium on the Theory of Computing, 1971.

B3   Bridgman, P.W., "An Operational Approach to Physics."

B4   Burstall, R.M., "Proving Properties of Programs by Structural Induction," *The Computer Journal*, 1969.

C1   Chomsky, N., "Formal Properties of Grammars," *Handbook of Mathematical Psychology 2*, Wiley, 1963.

C2   Church, A., *The Calculi of Lambda Conversion*, Princeton, 1941.

C3   Constable, R., and Borodin, A., "Subrecursive Programming Languages," to be published in the *JACM*.

C4   Curry, H., and Feys, R., *Combinatory Logic*, North Holland, 1958.

D1   Dennis, J.B., and Patil, S., "Computation Structures," notes for M.I.T. Course 6.232, 1970.

D2   Dijkstra, E., "An ALGOL 60 Translator for the XI Computer," *ALGOL Bulletin Supplement No. 10*, 1960.

F1   Falkoff, A.D., K.E. Iverson, and E.H. Sussenguth, "A Formal Description of System/360," *IBM Systems Journal 3*, No. 3, 1964.

F2   Floyd, R.W., "Assigning Meanings to Programs," Proc. Symp. Appl. Math., *AMS*, Vol. 19, 1967.

F3   ——, "Syntactic Analysis and Operator Precedence," *JACM*, 1963.

F4   ——, "Bounded Context Syntactic Analysis," *CACM*, 1964.

G1   Ginsburg, S., *The Mathematical Theory of Context-Free Languages*, McGraw-Hill, 1966.

H1   Hartmanis, J., and Stearns, R.E., *Algebraic Structure Theory of Sequential Machines*, Prentice-Hall, 1966.

H2   Henhapl, W., and Jones, C.B., "The Block Structure Concept and Some Possible Implementations with Proofs of Equivalence," IBM Lab., Vienna, TR 25.104, 1970.

H3   Hoare, C.A.R., "Proof of a Program FIND," *CACM*, January 1971.

H4   Hopcroft, J., and Ullman, J., *Formal Languages and Their Relation to Automata*, Addison-Wesley, 1969.

I1   Ianov, Iu.I., "The Logical Schemes of Algorithms," *Problems of Cybernetics* [USSR] 1, 1960.

I2   Irons, E.T., "Structural Connections in Formal Languages," *CACM*, February 1964.

J1   Johnston, J.B., "The Contour Model of Block Structured Processes," Symposium on Data

Structures in Programming Languages, *SIGPLAN Notices*, February 1971.

J2   Jones, C.B., and Lucas, P., "Proving Correctness of Implementation Techniques," IBM Lab., Vienna, TR 25.110, August 1970.

K1   King, J.C., "A Program Verifier," Ph.D. Thesis, Carnegie-Mellon University, 1969.

K2   Knuth, D.E., "On the Translation of Languages from Left to Right," *Information and Control*, December 1965.

L1   Landin, P.J., "The Mechanical Evaluation of Expressions," *Computer Journal 6, 4*, 1964.

L2   ——, "A Correspondence Between ALGOL 60 and Church's lambda notation," *CACM*, February and March 1965.

L3   Lauer, P., "Formal Definition of ALGOL 60," IBM Lab., Vienna TR 25.088, December 1968.

L4   Lucas, P., "Two Constructive Realizations of the Block Concept and Their Equivalence," IBM Lab., Vienna, TR 25.085, 1968.

L5   ——, et al., "Method and Notation for the Formal Definition of Programming Languages," IBM Lab., Vienna, TR 25.082, 1968.

L6   ——, and Walk, K., "On the Formal Description of PL/I," *Annual Reviews in Automatic Programming 6, 3*, 1969.

L7   Luckham, D.C., Park, D.M.R., and Paterson M.S., "On Formalized Computer Programs," *Journal of Computer and System Sciences*, June 1970.

M1   Manna, Z., "Properties of Programs and the First-Order Predicate Calculus," *JACM*, April 1969.

M2   ——, and Waldinger, R.J., "Towards Automatic

Program Synthesis," *CACM*, March 1971.

M3   McCarthy, J., *Towards a Mathematical Science of Computation*, IFIP Congress 1962, North Holland, 1963.

M4   ———, *A Formal Description of a Subset of ALGOL, Formal Language Description Languages*, North Holland, 1966.

M5   ———, and Painter, J., "Correctness of a Compiler for Arithmetic Expressions," Proc. Symp. Appl. Math., *AMS*, Vol. 19, 1967.

M6   ———, et al., *The LISP 1.5 Programming Manual*, M.I.T. Press, 1965.

M7   McGowan, C., "Correctness Results for Lambda Calculus Interpreters," Ph.D. Thesis, Cornell University, 1971; TR 71-34, Center for Computer and Information Sciences, Brown University, February 1971.

M8   ———, "The Correctness of a Modified SECD Machine," 2d ACM Symposium on the Theory of Computing, May 1970.

M9   ———, "An Inductive Proof Technique for Interpreter Equivalence," Courant Institute Symposium on Formal Semantics, September 1970.

M10   ———, and Wegner, P., "The Equivalence of Sequential and Associative Information Structure Models," Symposium on Data Structures in Programming Languages, *SIGPLAN Notices*, February 1971.

M11   Mendelson, E., *Introduction to Mathematical Logic*, Van Nostrand, 1964.

N1   Naur, P., et al., "Report on the Algorithmic Language ALGOL 60," *CACM*, May 1960.

N2   ———, et al., "Revised Report on the Algorithmic Language ALGOL 60," *CACM*, January 1963.

O1   Organick, E.I., and Cleary, J.G., "A Data Structure Model for the B6700 Computer System," Symposium on Data Structures in Programming Languages, *SIGPLAN Notices*, February 1971.

P1   Paterson, M.S., "Equivalence Problems in a Model of Computation," Cambridge University 1967, Available as M.I.T. Artificial Intelligence Memo No. 1, November 1970.

P2   Plato, *The Republic*.

R1   Randell, B., and Russell, L., *ALGOL 60 Implementation*, Academic Press, 1964.

R2   Rutledge, J., "On Ianov's Program Schemata," *JACM*, January 1964.

S1   Schoenfeld, J.R., *Mathematical Logic*, Addison-Wesley, 1967.

S2   Scott, D., "Outline of a Mathematical Theory of Computation," Proc. 4th Princeton Conference on Information Sciences and Systems, March 1970.

S3   Sethi, R., and Ullman, J.D., "The Generation of Optimal Code for Arithmetic Expressions," *JACM*, October 1970.

S4   Stearns, R.E., and Lewis, P.M., "Properties, Grammars and Table Machines," *Information and Control*, 1969.

T1   Tarski, A., "The Semantic Concept of Truth," *Philosophy and Phenomenological Research 4*, 1944.

W1   Walk, K., "Modelling Storage Properties of Higher-Level Languages," Symposium on Data Structures in Programming Languages, *SIGPLAN Notices*, February 1971.

W2   ——, et al., "Abstract Syntax and Interpretation of PL/I, Version III," IBM Lab., Vienna, TR 25.098, April 1969.

W3   Wegner, P., *Programming Languages, Information Structures and Machine Organization*, McGraw-Hill, 1968.

W4   ———, "Three Computer Cultures," *Advances in Computers 10*, Academic Press, 1970.

W5   ———, "Information Structure Models for Programming Languages," Center for Computer and Information Sciences, Brown University, September 1970.

W6   ———, "Data Structure Models for Programming Languages," Symposium on Data Structures in Programming Languages, *SIGPLAN Notices*, February 1971.

W7   ———, "The Vienna Definition Language," TR 70-21-2, Center for Computer and Information Sciences, Brown University, May 1970. To be published in *Computing Surveys*.

W8   ———, "The Semantics of Algebraic Languages," first draft of a monograph, April 1969.

W9   ———, "The Variability of Computations," TR 70-22, Center for Computer and Information Sciences, Brown University, July 1970.

CONSTRUCTIVE FORMALIZATION

A. van Wijngaarden
Mathematische Centrum, Amsterdam

The talk by Professor Wijngaarden was a tutorial explication of elements of ALGOL 68.

[1] Branquart, P., Lewi, J., Sintzoff, M., and Wodon, P.L., "The Composition of Semantics in ALGOL 68," *CACM*, November 1971.

[2] Lindsey, C.H., and van der Meulen, S.G., *Informal Introduction to ALGOL 68*, North Holland, 1971.

[3] Peck, J.E.L., ed., "ALGOL 68 Implementation," *Proceedings of the IFIP Working Conference on ALGOL 68 Implementation*, Munich, July 20-24, 1970. North Holland, 1971.

[4] van Wijngaarden, A., *Orthogonal Design and Description of a Formal Language*, MR 76, Mathematics Centrum, Amsterdam, 1965.

[5] ———, (ed.), Mailloux, B.J., Peck, J.E.L., Koster, C.H.A., "Report on the Algorithmic Language ALGOL 68," *Numerische Mathematic, 14*, 1969, pp. 79-218.